THE JUBILEE BOY

Also available in this series:

The Jubilee Boy

The life and recollections
of
George Swinford of Filkins

Researched and edited by

JUDITH FAY

and

RICHARD MARTIN

ISIS
LARGE PRINT
Oxford, England

First published in Great Britain 1987
by The Filkins Press

Published in Large Print 1994 by Isis Publishing Ltd,
7 Centremead, Osney Mead, Oxford OX2 0ES
by arrangement with The Filkins Press

British Library Cataloguing in Publication Data
Jubilee Boy: Life and Recollections of
George Swinford of Filkins. — New ed. —
(ISIS Reminiscence Series)
I. Fay, Judith II. Martin, Richard
III. Series
942.41708

ISBN 1-85695-116-2

Printed and bound by Hartnolls Ltd, Bodmin, Cornwall
Cover designed by CGS Studios Ltd, Cheltenham

CONTENTS

ACKNOWLEDGEMENTS

Throughout the long business of researching and editing *The Jubilee Boy*, we have had the help and support of innumerable people. George's family has answered all sorts of questions with unfailing courtesy. Betty Booth has been a tireless interpreter of manuscript notes and Shillbrook Office Services word-processed fast and furiously. Alison Goldingham cast her professional pencil over the typescript. The printing staff of Redwood Burn have greatly helped the fledgeling Filkins Press. Betty Booth and Jane Martin have shown great forebearance when we should have been doing something else.

Above all, we would like to thank George Swinford senior who has enthusiastically supported our efforts in expanding his original memoirs into *The Jubilee Boy*. We hope that this is more than just a record of the long life of an interesting man. As *The Jubilee Boy* went to press, George celebrated his hundredth birthday. At a village tree-planting to mark the event, he said that he hoped that everyone present would enjoy living in Filkins as much as he had and that they would live to be a hundred and plant a tree! We hope that any joy in *The Jubilee Boy* will illustrate why George thinks as he does, and why we agree with him. There are no intended villains in the story, only players in their particular hours; and any faults are ours.

Filkins 1987   **Judith Fay and Richard Martin**

FOREWORD

At his ninety-ninth birthday party George Swinford joined in heartily with the singing of "For he's a jolly good fellow!" As well he might. From his recollections, which he started writing in a steady, impeccable hand in a hard-backed exercise book on 11th December 1955, and finished when he reached the last line of the last page on 2nd February 1958, someone quite unique emerges.

Here is the man who spent the long, lonely evenings after the death of his first wife carving an elaborate four-poster bed for Lady Isobel Cripps. Ostensibly to show his gratitude to her for her help, was his careful shaping of the trees, birds and flowers of each season also a tribute to his wife and his mother, who had both weathered so many hard years?

Here, too, is the man who sat up to his knees in water in a dark dug-out during World War One, while the world around him was being blown to bits, meticulously engraving thirty-six match box covers from German shell cases for the men in his platoon, because non-safety matches could set one's pocket alight.

For George Swinford life was often harsh and painful. At the age of thirteen he worked eleven hours a day. "When I first started I was not always sure I could do it, as it was three miles to walk there, and so cold. Sometimes I shed a few tears and asked why I could not stay at home. Your boots were so stiff you had a job to get them on." At the worst of the slump George and his father cycled to Wales to find work, were told they were a fortnight too early, and cycled back home in time for an early breakfast. "It was a terrible time. Men in the streets out of work, hundreds of them."

But throughout his life George Swinford has carried in his mind the image of somewhere he calls Filkins, which he describes as "a little world in itself." A place where everything is made on the spot, it is peopled by busy, respected masons, blacksmiths, wheelwrights, carpenters, hurdle-makers, tailors and shoe-makers, as well as a brigade of indomitable, sometimes fiery wives and mothers who can turn their hand to anything. In George's mind they live on, along with the squire, schoolmaster, parson and doctor — now beneficent, now tyrannical — and, above all, his parents. "I often remember something else about my father when I'm going to bed," he said recently.

George is proud to take after his father, "sticking up for myself and for what's fair." A forthright man, hot for justice, Jo Swinford was always one for a joke; in this, too, George takes after him. Mother, who bore twelve children and was a good judge of pigs, was literally a tower of strength, six foot tall and seventeen stone in weight, a woman who thought nothing of baking ninety-one sparrows in a pie. "She was busy all right."

Father and Mother set a pattern of self-respect and persistence. At four years old George was hammering nail after nail into the toughest plank his father could find, and marching proudly to school murmuring: "It's a *bought* suit, not a made one." From his father, perhaps, came his dry, matter-of-fact turn of phrase: "The Coal Charities were for the old people, but sometimes the parson decided who was old." But his poetic way with words is his own. "I knew where good watercress grew, free from drainage." "One day when I was working, a nightingale in a hedge nearby was singing, fit to split the sky." "You would go to a piece of ground called Furzey to draw a faggot to hot your oven."

George Swinford's original document, which he called *The History of Filkins* and wrote over thirty years ago, is a piece of history in itself. It seems to have been prompted by his fascination at reading about the derivation of the name Filkins (a curious name which strangers sometimes doubt could refer to a real place). He was probably also inspired by Thomas Banting who had written an account of his life in Filkins during the early nineteenth century. George quotes from Thomas Banting in his own story.

George Swinford ended his recollections, on which this book is partly based: "It is now 2nd February 1958, and I am in my seventy-first year. I hope to write a few more stories, as I think of them, that might be interesting to someone in years to come." Today, in his hundredth year, he has just remembered how his grandmother poured toffee onto a special stone for it to set; it was generally peppermint-flavoured and sold at four ounces for a halfpenny. The stone may still be around somewhere, he thinks. Fireside reminiscences can still last two hours, and as George warms to his memories he peels off jacket, waistcoat and pullover. The small wood fire burns low, but the story-teller reaches for another log, and another lively incident.

CHAPTER
ONE

Beginnings

If I'm going to write about my life I should begin at the beginning. I was born on 17th July 1887 in the year of Queen Victoria's Golden Jubilee, on a Sunday morning. I have heard my father say that he went up to The Bull Inn at dinner-time to have a drink, and he told the other men there and this meant a few extra drinks, and being a very hot day they went and laid down in the shade of the trees up behind the town for the whole afternoon.

We lived in two cottages in Hazells Lane. We rented one for a shilling a week, the other was left to us by our uncle, Job Farmer. There were two bedrooms in each cottage. You slept in a truckle bed with another of the family, top to tail. My parents' big wooden bed did not have a mattress, just sacking laced up the sides, and of course it sagged in the middle. On top of that they had a featherbed to lie on, and very nice hand-sewn calico sheets and pillowcases, and proper blankets from Witney, which was where the blanket trade was famous. They had a washstand in the corner with jug and basin of thick earthenware. It looked like red china, but it was only glazed inside. The bowls and pans for the dairy and kitchen were from the same pottery at Charlbury. They were sent round by horse and cart from village to village. You could buy a chamber pot if you had the money, otherwise it was outside to the Vaults (as we called the earth closet) down the garden, even in the night.

You kept your everyday clothes hanging in the bedroom. Mother and Father had a curtain over theirs. Sunday clothes were folded tidy in a wooden chest with newspaper to keep the moths away. We did not have carpets then, just bare boards, with Mother's rag rugs. She would back them with sacking. I still have in the Museum the stag-horn needle which she used. She had a job keeping those rugs clean, with us all tramping in and out with our muddy boots. Mother was always washing the floor. It was amazing how people kept their houses clean, and managed to do so much work. Of course the first-born was always able to help the last-born.

Downstairs we had a few pictures on the walls, mostly embossed cards in memory of dead relatives. Father made wooden frames with crosses to form joints at the corners, as this was easier than using a mitre. Mother always kept the big table where we all sat to have our meals scrubbed white with soap and sand. The little round table in the corner had a single leg with three feet. It was polished and we were never allowed to touch anything on it. One thing was a stuffed quail, and our cat did not like that quail at all. Our neighbour's cat was called Moses, so Father said "We'll call ours Aaron." I also remember there was a central oak post with a swivel chair on it for the baby, so it could sit up to the table or look out of the window or face the fire. There was a potty underneath.

On the wall there was an old clock with a painted dial and pendulum and chains with weights hanging down. The top was rounded with a picture of the moon with horns on it. It looked rather like a Cotswold sheep, so people called it a "Sheep-head clock". When Father had to clean it because it had stopped he would take the works out and boil them in a saucepan, to get rid of the grease and dirt. He used to oil the clock with a goose feather. It went well on the whole. Everyone seemed to have a clock like that, until Mazawattee started putting coupons in the tea packets, and when you had saved up a great many you could send them up and get a clock with a black marble stand. I think these may have been the first coupons to be sent out in packages, as we had never seen them before.

A great many things in the home were made out of wood. For instance Mother's washtub, and the bowl she made the dough for the bread in, also the bowl she mixed the currant pudding in. We ate out of small wooden porringers. Father's shaving bowl was wooden, and so of course was the coal box by the fire. And my eleven brothers and sisters and I were all rocked in the same wooden cradle.

Outside our cottage we had a lovely rose, a Gloire de Dijon. It always came out at Whitsuntide, and on Whit Sunday we would sell the buds for a penny each.

As I said, there were twelve children in our family. My sister Millicent Harriet was eighteen months older than me, I came next, then Elizabeth Mary, Prudence Philippa, Alice, Elsie, James, Thomas, John, Edward, Jo and Fred. We were all born between 1885 and 1900. Fred, the youngest, was just too young for the War. I remember Father throwing his calling-up papers into the fire.

My mother said I was walking at nine months, and when I was twelve months my father made me a little wheelbarrow. It seems I had quite a lot of energy at that time. One day they lost me. When they found me I was down the village on the way to my grandmother's, sitting on my wheelbarrow swinging my legs. That was when I was about eighteen months, they said, but I do not remember it.

My father was very fond of carving. He would bring home bits of wood and whittle away at them, and of course I wanted to do it too. I was about four years old then and they were not going to trust me with a pocket knife, so my father got me a little hammer. I've still got it in the Museum. He would drive in a nail so far, and I would hammer it the rest of the way into the wood. I soon tumbled to it, and my father said I was driving them in too fast. "I can't keep up with thee!" So he got a six-inch nail and drove it in a bit. I hammered and hammered, but I couldn't get it in. I remember sitting on the rug, trying and trying. The big nail shone like silver in the firelight, and my father said "That's beat thee!"

We had a basket baby carriage, and I remember pushing my sisters in it. Seems like there was always a baby. We were well fed even though times were hard. My father said "Fill their bellies and their backs will look after themselves." I remember the babies' feeding-bottles. When rubber came in the bottle had a glass tube on the end of it, and when the tube got broken my father would go to what was called "the tea tree", and get a twig and push a wire through the middle to get the pith out. Then it was used to fit onto the rubber on the bottle instead of the glass tube. You can still see one of those "tea trees" growing out of the wall on the left-hand side before you get to the school.

We had few toys. The babies had basket rattles and bits of chain, and the little girls would sit by the fire pretending to knit. They soon learnt to do it properly, as everyone had to be handy with the needles. The wool came from Witney. Father made me my first cricket bat, and later I made them too, with the butts of willow trees. Very good they were — you see, the wood was just right. One time there were two boys staying in the village and they were playing cricket with a stick, so I made them a bat. Years later they came back and said "That bat you've made us, we've still got it."

I had a terrier called Tiny. He was too small for ratting, but I knew all the drains going across under the roads. Tiny went in one side after a rabbit, and I caught it in a bag the other side and pulled its neck — a quick job. Mother would cook a rabbit pie or stew for Sunday out of two or three rabbits, flavoured with bacon.

I knew every inch of the country, every tree and plant. I knew where good watercress grew, free from drainage, which we had as a treat for tea with bread and salt butter. Of course I knew where there were plenty of dandelions to make our dandelion wine. You would put your finger under and just pluck off the tops. We also collected hops — I do not suppose that any young people today know where hops grow, but I could show them.

We also made elderberry wine which we used to take

to work, but parsnip wine was the most common. Mother boiled it up and you kept it in three lots, the good, the better and the best. The best was kept the longest and was the strongest. Father always planted a big patch of parsnips, and Mother bought a hundredweight of sugar. First it was kept in big pans in the wash-house covered with a sheet, and you would peep in to see if it was working. Then you put it into quart vinegar bottles, or into wooden barrels which had held nine gallons of beer, and which we bought from a man for a few shillings. You had to keep quiet about them, as they were stolen. He should have sent them back.

Cooking was done in the iron cauldron and kettle, hung over the open fire with a crane and pothooks. Everything was cooked together. Potatoes and cabbage were boiled along with the bacon in string nets which the gypsies came round selling. Dumplings were boiled in the bacon broth, and the currant pudding, wrapped up tightly in a cloth and sealed with flour so the bacon taste did not get in, was cooked there too. We used two-pronged forks to eat with and knives with handles made of stag-horn. Our spoons were made of horn too, or of beechwood. I remember two graces.

He who blesses loaves and fishes
Look down upon these humble dishes,
Although they are but few and small
Thou knowest they're meant to fill us all,
And if our stomachs they do fill
Then thou hast wrought a miracle.

Some have meat and cannot eat,
Some can eat and have no meat,
We have meat and we can eat,
So the Lord make us thankful.

In fact we scarcely ever had meat in the way of beef or mutton except on feast days, although Mother had a jack for roasting meat on. It was almost always bacon, with a few hares, rabbits and small birds.

We had two pigs in March and two more at Michaelmas. Mother was a good judge of pigs, and did the buying. The pig butcher came round to each house to kill them. Neighbours exchanged pig-meat, as we did the killing at different times. They would give you a bit of bread or whatever they had for the pig, and after it was killed you would give them a fry-up in exchange. It was all well done, and everyone was satisfied.

The pigsty had to be fifty feet from the house, but that was not always possible. The pig had chiefly toppings, bran and barley meal. We had two allotments, one for vegetables for the family and one for barley for the pig. and we changed the one to the other each year. The barley was threshed with a flail in the big barn at Cross Tree. Later, when the threshing machine came in, each one put his barley in a separate pile, and the machine threshed it in turn.

After the pig was killed it was divided up. Every bit was used. There was backbone for backbone pie, spare-rib joints, sides of bacon, and of course collared head. I do not remember all the parts. The tail was important. It was cut off with quite a bit of fat left on it, and hung up to dry on the back of the door. Then when the snow was on the ground you would heat it up over the fire and rub it on your boots to soften them so that you could get them on, as they always dried stiff, and it also helped to keep the wet out. There were faggots, too, of course, and plenty of lard. Mother strained the lard off, and the bits left behind in the strainer were called "cruttons", and she made pies with them or mixed them with currants and raisins and put them in a roly-poly in a tight cloth, fastened with safety pins, to boil.

Pickled ham was the best. It was so tender it would break off in your hand. If Mother had a chance to buy a bit more for pickling she would do so. She pickled it in brown sugar, black pepper, different kinds of spices and old beer, and you rubbed in saltpetre, especially into the knucklebone. She rubbed it into each rasher and piled them on top of each other. Every day she reversed them and rubbed in more pickling mixture. She had a special pickling trough lined with lead, and it was kept upstairs under the bed. When the ham was ready you hung it on a wooden frame like a hurdle, fastened to the hooks on the beam in the kitchen, so you could let it down and cut a piece off when you wanted to. Lovely, it was, the last piece went quite yellow. Father used to come in and say "Come on now, let's have a slice of the yellow bacon." It has not been made since the War. It did not have so much fat on it, and you never got tired of it. It would only last us a week or two, then back on the old job — taters and bacon. One day I went to see an old friend, Jim, who was ill. I took him some pickled ham. and I said to his wife "Don't tell him." But he shouted down "Bring I up some of that yaller bacon", because he could smell it. The last bit of the pig to be used was its bladder, which we boys all wanted for a football.

We got some of our things at the local shops. There were three. One was Jeannette Farmer's shop, at the end of Rouse's Lane. It was very dark inside, and Miss Farmer could not see very well, so sometimes we would put our hand in the sweet jar while she was counting up the money. You bought a sweet there marked like a piece of streaky bacon, which cost a halfpenny and was called Hanky Panky. It was the custom for some families to take a London child for a week's holiday for five shillings, and as we had four bedrooms we could take an extra boy in, and he would get the usual bacon, taters, cabbage and rhubarb. One of our jokes was to send him into the shop for a pennorth of Yanky Doodle.

The biggest shop was by Broughton Bridge. It was a very busy place, the bell at the door was always ringing. There was tinned-meat — bully beef — but no tinned fruit then, just dried fruit. There was also bacon and lard for those who had no pig of their own. We got some of our things from the grocer at Clanfield who delivered in his van — sugar, tea, yeast, soda and sanitation stuff for the closet, and maybe a bit of jam sometimes. We settled with him once a year, as he had one of our pigs at Michaelmas. Mother would go back in the van with him after the pig was killed to see it being weighed up, so that we got the right money, which was generally sevenpence halfpenny a pound.

One day Mother went shopping in Witney with the younger children, and left me and my older sister Millie at home. At dinner-time Millie said "What are we going to have, just bacon?" I said "I'll go out and get us something." You see, I knew where some partridges had nested alongside the road, behind the stone planks which bounded the field. Planks were like slats, only thicker, and these had small trees and bushes growing among them. In those days the man who owned a field owned not only the wall or hedge too, but the grass verge and the road right up to the middle, where it met the land owned by the man with the field on the other side. So those partridges were the property of one of the farmers. I collected thirty-five partridge eggs and took them home, and Millie fried them with some bacon, and we ate them all. I remember how I enjoyed topping and opening each egg. They were very good. Then we said "What shall we do with the shells?", as we knew the farmer would miss the eggs and there would be trouble. In the end we put them down the Vaults (the outside closet). Now every winter on a moonlit night Father would empty the Vaults. It was always done at night, and we children had to stand around with lanterns to light him. A man came with a horse and cart and you loaded it on, and he took it to the allotments for a shilling a load. Some of it got emptied into ashpits (which were next to the Workhouse) and mixed up like mortar, to be shifted later. Everybody stayed at home the night you emptied the closet. Anyway, the next time Father did it there were the eggshells, floating about. He said "I wonder how they got there. Could a rat have got those eggs?" He did not say any more, but I think he guessed what had really happened.

Clothes were a problem, especially if you were a big family. When I was three or four they sold gaiters of shiny leather with a steel plate down the side at the Post Office, and I did so much want a pair. Father said "Let'm have 'em," so Mother gave me eighteen pence, which was quite a lot then. But when I got to the Post Office they only had one gaiter, not a pair. I took it and wore it and they did not take the money. As I got older, I wore Father's old clothes for years, cut down. One time while I was waiting for some new boots for several weeks I had to wear a pair of Father's old ones which were much too big. Mother was a very good needlewoman, and made all our clothes herself. Every Christmas Squire Fox's mother at the big house at Bradwell Grove gave all the women a Christmas box. There is an entry in the School Log Book, dated 11th December 1896, "A great many children away this afternoon chiefly because their mothers are gone to Bradwell Grove for gifts." You could choose if you would have sheets or blankets or a dress length. Mother always chose material. The one thing she wanted was a sewing machine, that was what she had *got* to have, and she was going to get it even though it cost five pounds. Of course Father had not got five pounds, so she worked for a farmer, haymaking and harvesting, and she saved that five pounds and got her sewing machine. A Singer treadle, it was. She was sewing every night after dark, and my sisters had to do a bit too. We only had candles for a long time. It was wonderful when we got our first paraffin lamp.

The Rummage Sales were exciting places those days.

The women used to fight each other over the dresses. Mother was always collecting pieces for her rag rugs, and one day Squire Fox's hunting coat was in the sale. There was a good scramble, but Mother got it, and after that there was always a piece of red in the middle of each rug, and sometimes at the corners too. We also had the gold buttons — W.H.F. they had on them, for William Henry Fox. Lovely buttons they were.

Squire Fox's father Samuel Fox invented Paragon umbrellas. They were the first ones with steel frames, the ones before having cane or whalebone frames. His factory was in Sheffield. He must have made a mint of money out of those umbrellas. It was said that he left three hundred and three thousand pounds in his Will. Squire Fox's mother was very good. She would invite the women of Filkins, Shilton and Bradwell Grove to go to tea with all the young children. We had a lovely tea party, bread and butter, cake and lettuce (lettuce was very special). Then at six o'clock the butler would bring in the beer in copper jugs. After that they would start walking home, chattering and singing, with the babies in the prams and us older children walking beside. We used to wonder why some of the women fell down on the way back.

Mother took her corn to the miller to have it ground, and as we did not have an oven in our house she and another woman combined to make the bread. When the bread for the week was finished, she would make a dough cake in the tin with lard and currants and candied peel, and you always took a good big bit of it with you when you went off from home. We all worked on the allotment with the vegetables. Mother would get the babies stuck in the pram asleep, and then she went home for the meal. My job was to make the fire and hang the kettle on a special stand the blacksmith made, which I have still got in the Museum. Mother also did the weeding and kept the bonfire going, and she would lay out the potatoes in a row in the trench. She was busy all right.

Another thing Mother did was to go wooding with the other women. They took trucks or prams or whatever they had got and went into the Squire's woods to pick up chippings from the axe. They had to work pretty fast because they must keep out when the pheasants were laying, or at other times when the keeper said. When you went wooding you would take a well-hook, which was used to draw the bucket of water out of the well, and sit on a branch and hook the rotten wood down. And when anyone was cutting a hedge we would go with bags to collect up the small wood.

For our washing we had a well like every other cottage, but it was not a spring, just surface water. The closet was a hole in the ground and it was not far from the house, nor was the pigsty, but it did not seem to do us any harm, as we never got ill except for measles. When the wells ran dry in August everyone had to fetch water from the brook down at Town Pool. My father got the wheels off an old horse-rake and made a barrow with two shafts and then all the men in our lane fetched the water together. Each of us had a yoke with two wooden buckets hanging, and so that the buckets did not spill out while you were walking Father made wooden crosses to float on top of them. Some of the men took turns pulling Father's barrow. It was a Sunday morning job, each one filling up all the tubs and buckets ready for Monday washday. By the time the men got home they were very thirsty as well as sweating, and Mother gave them her home-made parsnip beer to quench their thirst, with the result that they ended up very sleepy as well.

You had a bath on the rug in front of the fire. It was rather awkward if the others had not yet gone to bed. The copper where we did our washing was where Mother made her parsnip beer. I went on making it myself for many years, up till the time my wife died. Mother also made sloe wine. We called the sloes "slaws", and you picked them early in September, as the wine got muddy if they were over-ripe. We did not make our own cider, although John Garne at Manor Farm made plenty, having apple orchards and a horse to turn the wheel of the press. He always had a huge cider barrel, and would give anyone who called a drink. For the cottages a man went round from one to the other with a travelling mill. Blessed if I can remember exactly how he made the cider pulp! He had a wooden contraption with a piece of netting folded over and over. If you smashed the apples with a wooden mallet, you did not get the kernels, but if a village had a stone trough everyone could use it, and got the juice from the kernels which was a great improvement.

Mother made rhubarb jam, as it was good for your insides. We had apples and nuts and a few pears, not a lot. As for vegetables, there were plenty of potatoes of course and always cabbage. By cabbage I mean all green stuff, like brussels sprouts. We had carrots and parsnips, but not a lot of swedes or turnips. The farmers grew those for the sheep. If you wanted a turnip or two you had to ask the farmer. You had to be careful how you asked, and you had to be grateful. He would always say "Just a few, mind you, don't take too many". And when you wanted to burn the bristles off the pig after it was killed, you had a job to get a bundle of straw off the farmer. Father often had to ask for someone else who could not ask for himself for some reason. Some people got the bristles off with boiling water, but then you had to get the sticks to make the fire to heat the water, so it came to the same thing in the end.

My mother was six feet tall and weighed seventeen stone. She worked sometimes at Langford Mill, and the farmer weighed all the women on the scales he weighed sacks on. They turned the hay for him, and when it was ricked they had tea. Then they had singing, and at eight o'clock they had beer.

Three of my sisters died as babies before they were three weeks. They died of vaccination. Their arms swelled up and the scab went right over the top of their heads. I remember taking them out in the pram like that. I suppose any calf was used, and some were not good enough for the job. After the third baby Father said he was not going to have it done again. At first you had to go to prison if you refused vaccination, but by that time you could appeal to the magistrate and get a paper for three and sixpence. My father appealed, and one of the magistrates was the doctor himself. He said "Why are you objecting?" and my father said "You ought to know. You vaccinated them." I know where they are all buried, five of them, as two more died of pneumonia. We children always went to the funeral. The little coffin was painted silver and carried in a big handkerchief, with Mother one side and another woman on the other. They did not have a headstone. Although we were Methodists they had to be buried in the Church of England, and christened too. It was not until later that the Methodists could do their own christenings, marriages and funerals.

Mother was very poorly when Jack was born, and either she or the boy was expected to die. She was bad for a whole month and the doctor's bill was mounting up, so she said to him "Don't come any more. I can manage all right now." But he said "I shall call when I want to, and I shan't ask you." Mother said "How much do I owe you?" "Seven and six." Mother said "I'll get it" and she did, and gave it to him when he next came. He picked it up and handed it back, saying "Get yourself something nice." He was the same doctor who had vaccinated the babies. Father was away at the time, building part of a vicarage at Lower Bourton, and living in lodgings. There was no telephone then, of course, only telegrams for news. Father asked the vicar if he would let them send a telegram there if the news was worse, and he said "Of course". And every Saturday when Father came home the vicar's wife sent a parcel of cakes and sweets.

A lot of young children died. I think the doctors were not too particular if one or two in large families went. I suppose it made sense, in a way. Plenty of families in Filkins had twelve or fourteen children. I wonder how some of them managed to get indoors. In the School Log Book, the following entries were made —

11th January 1897	Two cases of measles.
15th January	A sudden change for the worse in the health of the children, there being twenty-four away today.
18th January	Much illness in the village, and the school closed.
19th January	School closed for one month by order of the Medical Officer.
26th February	Work in school is a good deal impeded just now by persistent coughing.
10th March	There are now from 10 to 12 children away daily, some for an affliction of the eyes, others for eruptions.
15th April	We are not making satisfactory progress yet, the debility following measles and chickenpox the apparent cause.
11th May	The ill effects of the long illnesses are now passing.

Once there was an outbreak of typhoid in Fulbrook, just beyond Burford, so we boys had to carry a piece of carbolic soap in our pockets and have tarred rope wound round our legs as protection.

We did not have a dentist in the village, but the vet pulled teeth. He lived in my present cottage after the maltster had moved out. When he had finished the job he threw the bowl of water over the wall into the field. Years later when I dug up that part to add to my garden, I found any number of teeth in the ground. One had quite a large part of jaw on it. Rough times! I remember when I was ten years old and had toothache. I went to dance and feast at Queen Victoria's Diamond Jubilee at Broughton Hall with my face in a big handkerchief. My father gave me sixpence to go to the vet to have my tooth out, but when I got there I decided against it, and went to the shop and bought a pocket-knife with the sixpence instead. The toothache must have got better somehow.

CHAPTER
TWO

Good Times, Bad Times

They talk about "the good old days", but I am not sure about that. There were three things worse then than they are now, bad living conditions, poor food and no clothes. A pair of shoes for one of the family cost ten shillings, and that was a farm labourer's whole week's wage.

Times were especially hard for old people. There were thirteen cottages down Rouse's Lane where the old people who were on the Parish lived. They got sixpence a week and a loaf of bread. The bread was delivered by a man in a horse and trap, but he would not drive up the lane, so the old people had to come down as best they could on their sticks. My father complained about this, and after that the man drove up and called at each house. Old men working at Oxleaze Farm would have nothing but a drop of tea made out of a burnt crust, and often no food at all. If the farmer they were working for had no swedes or turnips, they would have to steal from the next farm. They would take one to eat on the way and one in the basket for dinner. A turnip grown for the sheep — that was all they had to eat. The farmer was always watching, and he would summons a man for stealing one turnip or swede. Walking was a job for them too as those boots that cost a whole week's wage were as much as you could lift.

I remember an old woman called Granny Clack, who lived in a thatched cottage not far from our house. I used to go in and chop her some wood, or get her some kindling up the hedges. I do not know what she lived on, but I remember sitting on a stool talking to her, and she would fetch a little dish with a bit of pudding in it and say "Eat this, George." I did not know what it was made of and I did not think much of it, but I would eat it all the same. I used to like going to have a talk with this old woman, and I do remember how poor she was.

People shifting around would not have a pig of their own, and that was a great disadvantage. There were six farm cottages at Cross Tree for casual labourers. Terrible places they were, in very poor repair, with no water. The people there would get into a bad state, ill and lousy, and then the farmer would sack them and they had to go back to the hiring fair at Burford to get another job. The men would all be lined up there. The carter would wear a bit of whipcord in his coat or hat, the shepherd some wool, the cowman a cow's tail, and the groom, who was gardener too, a bit of sponge. The farmer would look them up and down. "That looks a fairish strongish chap. Where were you working? Why did you leave?" The man would not say he had been kicked out, of course, but he had to think of something or other. At that time the farmer did not sign anything, so there was no proper agreement or wage settled. He would just promise to fetch the man and his family in a waggon at Michaelmas. When the waggon came with a little straw in it, they would put their bundle of things in, and any bits of furniture or bedding. Nothing was under cover, and if it rained it was a poor job. They did not know what sort of place they were coming to. I have seen women outside those Cross Tree cottages crying and saying "I'm not stopping here!" But they could not get out of it. Their friends might be five miles away, so they lost touch with them. It was a nasty business. After 1914 the hiring fairs were over, and instead they printed an advertisement form, and a bill of agreement was signed. I have one in the Museum.

We were better off because our family had been skilled workers in the building trade for generations. My great-great grandfather came from the village of Chalford, near Stroud, in Gloucestershire. He was a builder, and he came to Filkins quarry, which was worked by Mr Farmer, and married his daughter and settled down here. I do not know much about the two earlier generations, but I have heard a lot about my grandfather, although I did not know him. His name was Joseph, and he was a mason and a good craftsman. He was helping to build the stone railway bridges between Oxford and Shipton-under-Wychwood. When building the bridge between Hanborough and Combe he was lifting a large stone, and was said to have burst a blood vessel which caused his death. He was buried on a Saturday, and the next day, Sunday, my father was born.

My grandmother Rachel Swinford, was left with two sons and a daughter, and she had a great struggle to bring them up. She worked very hard. She would scrub out the bakehouse from five in the afternoon till ten at night, and got one loaf for it. Then she went into service with the Colston family at Filkins Hall, and when the house burnt down and they moved to Bournemouth she went with them. My father used to tell us a story about how one day he and my Uncle George, his older brother, went to Bournemouth to see her, and they went out in a boat. Uncle George had never seen the sea. He sat in the boat with his back to the shore, and after about an hour's voyage he said to my father "Jo — when are we going to start?"

We were quite a big family. My mother's mother had three husbands, and her father had two wives. Her name was Jane Belinda Willis, and she married my father in 1886. Her father, George Willis, was a slater and plasterer, also a lath-renderer.

My father was born in 1864. He was twenty-three years old when I was born, and he died in 1952 at the age of eighty-eight. When he first went to school two big boys had to carry him in, and he ran away ever so many times. He was always independent. He was working at Squire Fox's house at the time of the election, and as the Squire was a strong Tory at election times he would arrange for a waggon and horses to take the men he employed to vote. My father refused to go, because he was voting Liberal. The other men said "Squire won't like it," but he would not go with them. He went home and had his tea, and then he walked across the fields on his own to vote. He was not bound to the Squire.

We had our own cottage, and that was the main thing, as we could not be turned out. Squires had a lot of power in those days. If you lived in one of their houses, you had to keep your mouth shut. I think I take after my father, and that was why I got into trouble at school. I was not meaning to be naughty, just sticking up for myself and for what was fair, as he did.

One of the early things I can remember when I must have been about five or six years old was my father sitting in a chair with two black eyes, holding his arm and in a very bad humour. I asked Mother what was the matter with Dad, as he said very little and would not play with me. Mother said he had been fighting, and some men had got him down and kicked him. In later years I found out that he had been to Lechlade market, and had fallen out with a man named Shep Hayden. They had a fight in the yard of The Swan, and Dad came off best. He stayed in Lechlade drinking until ten o'clock, and then started home. When he got to the station bridge three men were there waiting for him and gave him a good hiding, leaving him there until someone came along and got him home.

Father was very fond of flowers, and we always had them growing by the house. There were not so many sorts then as now, and they were not so big, the pansies no bigger than violets. Father bought me a packet of pansy seeds and I grew them, and that is where I think my love of gardening started. My great-uncle Job was a fine gardener, and my father took after him. He won the cup three years running, so then he could keep it. It was given for the flower garden, the allotment and the general order of the whole. He beat the big gardens like Filkins Hall and Broughton Hall, and they employed gardeners. If you go to the holly tree on the corner of Cross Tree, where our second family home was (after we moved from Hazells Lane), you should imagine a double row of begonias. Beautiful begonias my father grew, and auriculas, too, which were brought over from France by the miners who worked there. "Bagers" they called them, and that is what my father called them. He had iron pots of them all round the top of our well. He grew a special green one, and when anyone left home they always had to take a cutting. He said their leaves were like mouse's ears.

When we were not at school (which I shall come to later) we were always busy. In those days, every man was a poacher. It was the only way. Rabbits, hares, partridges, pheasants — we caught blackbirds too, and sparrows. Broughton Hall was a good place, as the ivy on the wall was full of sparrows. When you clapped they all flew into the net, and so it was called a clapnet, a great big thing which had to be spread out and held by several boys. One night we caught ninety-one sparrows. Mother made a sparrow pie, and we boys took off our jackets and rolled up our sleeves and got down to it. A lot of people had not got Mother's gift for making things.

But we were not only interested in eating birds. I remember lying on my back as a boy in a field, listening to the larks singing overhead. There do not seem to be so many larks around Filkins these days. I think the severe winter frosts have killed them off. Up by the quarry a magpie used to build every year, and we used to fight over who should have the young to keep in a cage. Up at the Pills where there were lovely springs, Mr Kynaston from Oxleaze Farm put a water wheel in. The roof was not very high, and another gang of boys, not us, took the slates off to get at a starling's nest. The Sunday after that we were up there, and the cowman who was getting the cows in saw us and told the farmer, who got on his horse and started to chase us. We ran up the sides of the hedges, so he got the village policeman. We parted into two or three gangs and settled not to run away if we saw the policeman, but just quietly to say, "It wasn't we." But we had a deaf and dumb boy with us, Tommy Flux, and of course he could not hear what we had settled, so when he saw the policeman off he ran! We ran all round Broughton Hall, the farmer chasing us across the lawns on his horse. I and another boy laid in the manger in one of the stables and they did not see us. By six-thirty we were home for tea, and they did not catch any of us. Lucky it was, as it happened, as before the farmer first saw us we had caught one of his rabbits, and I had it in my pocket. During the chase I hid it in the long grass, and after it got dark I went and fetched it.

We boys always used to look out for jobs. The doctor came to the village on Tuesdays and Fridays, sometimes on horseback and sometimes in a high trap. While he was visiting, someone had to hold his horse. We got a penny for this. Sometimes we were late for school, but if we said we had been holding the doctor's horse all was well. On Wednesdays and Saturdays someone had to fetch the medicines from Burford, and when I was seven years old I started to do this and was allowed Wednesday out of school for it. I used to start from home about 6.30 am as the surgery hours were 8 am to

9 am. The doctor would come out into the waiting-room and ask "Have you had any breakfast?" and when I said "Yes thank you Sir", he would say "Could you eat some more?" and I would say "Yes thank you Sir", and he would tell me to leave my basket in the surgery. Then he would take me by the ear into the kitchen, and tell the cook to give me a good meal.

After getting the medicines packed up in the basket with the towels I took for the purpose, I would start back towards home, looking at the shops coming up Burford hill and seeing lots of things I would like. Toward Signet my basket began to get heavy, but I kept plodding on. I remember meeting the first motor car I ever saw, coming from Burford toward Signet. When I heard the noise, I wondered what it was. I gave it plenty of room to go by, and the two men in it laughed at me. I used to do a lot of birds-nesting on my way to and from Burford, which made the journey more interesting. Sometimes I got a lift on a waggon which was a great help, as it was five miles each way. I arrived back at Filkins about eleven o'clock, and then I would deliver the medicines. I got twopence a bottle, but sometimes if I had some for the big houses I would get sixpence. These bottles were specially wrapped in paper and sealed with sealing wax. I used to keep back twopence, unknown to Mother, to buy sweets, the rest she had, which was very welcome in those days. I did this journey twice a week until I left school and went to work.

I remember one day I set off from home as usual on a Wednesday. My mother had cut me two thick slices of bread off a four pound loaf (you do not get them that size nowadays) and spread it thick with lard and sprinkled sugar on it, and I had it in my basket with the lid fixed down with a wooden peg. I was passing the woods at Bradwell Grove where there were some holes left where the stones had been taken for building. As it was the end of autumn the holes were filled up with dead leaves, which we used to fetch in bags to make leaf mould for our plants. Suddenly the leaves in one big hole began to move, and out came a woman. She was all covered with leaves, and she shook herself like a dog. And then came two girls, aged about nine and ten. I felt frightened, but she said quietly "Don't be afraid, I won't hurt you." Although she was quite properly dressed I could see that she must be very poor, and I wondered how ever she and the children could have spent the whole night in a hole in the woods when it was nearly winter. So I opened my basket and took out the two slices of bread and gave them to her. She would not eat any herself, but gave it all to the children. Then we walked the road together, and when we got to the turning to Signet she showed me a cottage which had smoke coming out of the chimney, where she thought she could get a cup of tea. The last I saw of her was standing on the doorstep, waving to me. I have often wondered what became of her.

Another job I had was in the holidays, helping my uncle with the stick and fagging hook. I was eight or nine. You laid a handful of bonds and pulled it to your leg. But I kept chasing rabbits or lying watching the larks, so my uncle gave me the sack, and my sister took on the job instead. I well remember working with the fagging hook and stick. Only five miles from Filkins they were called reaping hook and crookstick.

There was always something to do. Sometimes William Morris came driving along the road from Kelmscott across the fields in his high carriage with his wife and two daughters. When we heard his horse clip-clopping, we boys ran to close the gate and stood waiting nearby. When he got there he would raise his whip and shout "You young rascals again!" but he always threw us a penny for opening the gate.

Then you got a farthing for fetching Fanny Farmer half an ounce of snuff which cost twopence farthing from the shop. You got a penny for carting half a hundredweight of coal in a wheelbarrow made by Sidney Imms' father, and another penny for taking it to be mended if the wheel came off, which was quite often, and you also got a ride back in it. Another job was to take the pony belonging to Philip Price, who lived then in my present house, to graze for an hour in a nice little field by the old mill. There was also an old chap with a mule, and he would give us a penny to graze him up the Kencot road, and we would have a ride on him.

I had a lot of jobs to do to help Mother in the house. I would scrape the grease off the candlesticks (that was before we got oil lamps) and shine them up, and the knives and forks as well. I also had to clean the family's boots. You used Ross's Blacking. A drop of vinegar mixed in, if you could get hold of it, made the leather shine better. I did not like the look of that tin of Ross's. It was the only word I had seen with three "esses" in it.

Of course it was not all work, and we spent some

of our time playing. We were fond of throwing stones, a pastime which seems to have died out nowadays. In my early years we always carried stones in our pockets, ready for anything that was considered a good target. Many a bird I have knocked off a branch, or a rabbit out of its set. There were champions at stone-throwing in every village. Our champion was Thomas Cook, who threw a stone from the road in front of the church across Clark's field onto the Kencot road, also Bill Dyer who stood on Broadwell Bridge and threw a stone over the weathercock on the church steeple. A story I heard many times was that when the farmers were having a shoot they employed Bill Dyer as beater. A hare jumped up, the gunners had four shots at him and did not stop him. He ran along about fifty feet from Bill, who picked up a stone and threw it at him, and as he remarked, cut him over as clean as a whistle.

We used to have our slings, too, you never see those now, they were a bit dangerous. We used to throw up at the rooks' nests with these slings, and I have seen the birds knocked out. To make a sling we would cut the tongue from one of our boots and buy a knot of whipcord. Some damage was done at times, and our parents took the slings away from us, but we soon managed to make another, which we kept out of sight. Very few of us had a catapult, as it was a job to get the elastic.

The games of marbles I played as a boy seem forgotten now. One game was Follow Tawl. A tawl was a special marble you used in most games, perhaps it was a large one or a bright one you knew from the rest. The glass ones were called glassies, the small ones were called cots. On the way to school we used to meet near The Bull Inn and shoot our way to school. Follow Tawl was played by shooting down the ruts made by the cart-wheels. You started by throwing a tawl in the rut. The one who was behind had the first shot, and if he hit the tawl he had a cot. Whoever was behind him had the next shot, and if he hit the tawl the first one had to give him the cot. It was surprising how many you could win or lose before you got to school.

Another game we played was Knock-Off. Each of us put one cot on a line under a wall, and then a mark was made where to stand. The first thrower tried to lob his tawl and knock as many cots off the line as he could. If he missed he could pick up his tawl and wait for his turn to come round again. If he knocked off one or more cots he picked them up, but he had to leave his tawl where it stopped. Then the next player had to give him the cots he had just won, and was out of the game. After the line was broken, that is when some of the cots had been knocked off, each player had to leave his tawl where it stopped, and the following player could either play on the tawl or on the cots. If he played on a tawl and hit it the owner would be out of the game, and if he was the last player and any cots were left on the line, he claimed them all. But if a player knocked off all the cots the next player had a go, and if he could hit the other player's tawl, that player had to give up all the cots he had just won, and the game was finished.

Another game we played was Ring Tawl. This was played on the road or any level place. A ring was drawn in the dust, and any number could play, the more players the larger the ring. When shooting, each player had to keep his hand firm on the ground. We used to say —

> Knuckle down, knuckle down,
> All four fingers touch the ground.

The thumb and forefinger were used only, and no punching! I have seen ten or fifteen games going on at one time near The Lamb Inn on a summer evening. Old men played as well as young, and some of them could shoot, too.

Then there was Top Spinning. The whip was a favourite game, which was played on the way to school. We used to see who could go the furthest down the road at one whip. The peg top was not used so much, as you wanted a hard surface to spin it on. This top you wound up with a piece of string with a loop around your forefinger, holding it between your thumb and finger with the point upwards. Then you threw it on the floor, pulling the string at the same time. If you landed them right they would hum and spin for a long time. I have heard of men who could spin one on top of another that was already spinning, but I have never seen it done myself.

We also had hoops. I have run a good many miles with a hoop. Our blacksmith would make one for a shilling, with hook and handle, about two feet six inches in diameter, and half an inch thick in round iron. You pushed them along with an iron hook, instead of beating them. We ran races with them, and it was good exercise on the cold days. Another thing we tried to do was to run a smaller one through a larger one when it was running along. It took some good judgement to do it, but I have seen it done.

Bandy was a game we played before football came to the villages. It was something like hockey. We used to cut sticks from the hedges with a knob or bend at the bottom. Instead of a ball we had a round chunk of wood about the size of a golf ball, which we called a nunney. We did not have any goals, but knocked it from one hedge to the other. The two captains picked up teams and started the game something like they do in hockey. Of course we had no idea about positions, we all ran to where the nunney was.

If you stood with your back in another's stomach to keep him off the nunney, he could shout "Turn, Bummy!" and if you did not move he could hit you with his stick, which used to cause some trouble. This was the only rule I can remember. You could kick, throw, trip, hold or anything you liked. I have seen some rough times at this game, but we used to enjoy it.

I have not written about the games which the girls played, but I must mention a few. They did not play robust games like the boys, but they did a lot of skipping, played ring-a-roses and hopscotch, and they had their wooden hoops just as the boys had their iron ones. They also did some simple dancing. I remember the older girls having a long pole with a large bunch of flowers on top, going round to the big houses and saying a verse first, then swinging the garland up and down. Afterwards they sang songs, for which they got a few coppers. The verse was —

Good morning, good Ladies and Gentlemen,
We wish you a happy day,
We have come to show you our garland,
Because it is the day;
Garlands above,
Garlands below.
See what a maypole we can show.

Valentine's Day was remembered for sending cards.
I remember the girls forming a ring and surrounding a
boy if they could. Then they would say this verse —

Good morning, Valentine,
I'll be yours if you'll be mine,
If no apples you can find,
Please to give us a bacon chine.

Then the girls would close in and try to kiss him.

We did enjoy the occasional outing, especially to
the Fairs. Lechlade was the Horse Fair, but it also
had amusements and stalls selling things. One day
(September 9th, I believe) we were all lessing in the
field opposite the East Leach turn, my mother and Mrs
Willis and Mrs Tooley, and all the babies and prams and
younger children. Someone passing said "It's Lechlade
Fair today." One said "Let's go", and another "Why
not!" "We *will* go, then." Mother went back home to
get dinner for everybody — bacon, peas and potatoes.
We all had a jolly good dinner, then put on our best
clothes and walked to Lechlade. A little gang, we were,
each family had five or six children.

At the Fair there was a wild beast show — it was one

33

lion, called The Untameable. We met friends, did a lot of talking and had a cup of tea. There were roundabouts and swingboats and peepshows, one penny each. There were sweet stalls with rock, not sticks like today, but round (more like a stone, but not exactly). At about six or seven o'clock we all walked home, the babies asleep in their prams or their mothers' arms, the older children still jumping about, and there might be some singing.

Best of all were the special feast days and celebrations. I was born in 1887, the Golden Jubilee year and I was ten years old at the Diamond Jubilee, which I remember quite well. The schoolchildren all met at the school at about ten o'clock in the morning, and we were told to bring a flag if we had one, or a red or white or blue piece of rag to carry in the processions. We started from the school singing patriotic songs round the village, and finally up to the back of Filkins Hall, then in ruins. There were tables and seats, and a horse and trap arrived from the bakehouse with joints of meat, and these were put all along the tables with vegetables, pickles, etc., etc. and two large barrels of beer on a stand. Mr Garne, the farmer, was the leading figure, as he had given a fat sheep. He shouted "Will you all take your seats please, and I hope you have all brought your plate, knife and fork and cup, and I hope you will all have a good dinner and enjoy yourselves in the sports afterwards. Now I will ask the vicar to say grace." After this everyone sat down, and the people appointed to do the carving got busy. The beer was brought around in water cans, and the gingerbeer in large jugs. What a meal! A lot of people ate more than they needed, and by night had drunk more than they could carry, but from what I can remember everyone was happy, and talked about the wonderful meal they had on Jubilee Day, which was a rare thing in those days for so many.

After the meal Mr Garne got up and asked everyone to drink the health of our dear old Queen Victoria, and he said more, but I can't remember what, then the Vicar got up and said a few words, thanking all who had given money and food for this occasion. We all stood and sang the National Anthem, then three cheers for Mr Garne, the Vicar and several more.

Then we began to get ready for the sports. There were plenty of entries. The women had running, jumping and tug-of-war as well as the men, and of course the children. There were several heats of slow and fast bicycle riding, all using the same four cycles. I remember the tug-of-war for men and all the shouting and what a time it lasted, as they were so evenly matched.

While the sports were going on the tapsters were busy drawing beer for anyone who took their cup along. About six o'clock it was announced that there was still plenty of meat, bread and cheese for anyone who would like to have it, and the beer and gingerbeer were holding out very well, so everyone went and had what they wanted. Next day the food that was left over was divided amongst the larger families, and the men went and collected up the tables etc., and finished the beer which was given for this occasion by the brewers. So this ended the great day of the Diamond Jubilee of 1897. I have heard the story of it from people older than myself. I should add that I myself had toothache, with my face tied up in a big handkerchief, but it did not spoil the enjoyment.

Another big day of course, was Christmas — and how different it was when I was a small boy. How we looked forward to hanging up our stockings, and how excited we were with the contents, which were an orange, a sugar mouse, a sugar pig and a penny tin whistle or trumpet. For breakfast we had bacon fried with half an egg and mashed potatoes, for dinner ham and vegetables and plum pudding, for tea we had salt buttered toast and cake, and for supper ham again. All this food was very special, and different from usual. We had one book in our house, *The Family Herald* I think it was called, and on Christmas Day we were allowed to see the pictures in it, we thought this a great honour. In the evening we sat round a nice fire and roasted crab apples on the hot bars of the grate and ate them with nuts. I would mention that in the autumn we used to go and get crabs, take them home and fill a box, put them under the bed and keep them until Christmas. We also gathered hazelnuts and beechnuts, which had to be kept in tins so the mice could not get at them.

On Christmas Day we always had to go to Sunday School, and marched in line to church. When we came out the teachers marched us into the vicarage, in single file. At the door stood the Vicar and his wife, and as we passed by each one had a penny and an orange. As I got older I used to go round singing carols, and collected a few coppers. If the weather had not been too bad and Father had not been out of work, or if the fat pig they had just sold had done well, we could buy some extras, but it was not very often we got away from bacon.

Mostly we ate home cured lard instead of butter as long as it lasted, but we could buy salt butter for one shilling per pound at the farm. You could see the salt in it when you cut it, and it was very good for toast, and that is what we enjoyed for Christmas tea. Later years we used to have a football match on Christmas Day, which was very much appreciated after the Christmas dinner. Now there is nothing doing except a walk.

The first Boxing Day I remember there was rabbit-coursing in The Lamb field called The Gassons. Wild rabbits were caught in nets and brought in boxes. All the dogs were sorted out and put in pairs about the same size as one another, then a man showed the rabbit to the dogs and walked about ten yards away. When all was ready he shouted "Go!" and let the rabbit loose, and the dogs were unleashed and away they went. Sometimes the rabbit did not get very far, and sometimes he managed to get over the wall into the big common. Then we boys joined in the chase, and the one that caught the rabbit kept it. There were always a lot of gamekeepers and police at this event to see the dogs run, as it gave them the information they wanted — they found out who were good dogs for poaching, and the owners of these dogs. There were always a lot of gypsies there, and if the gamekeepers and police were around they did not run their best dogs, but kept them in the trap or cart out of sight, and only ran their young dogs. I think the last rabbit coursing was held about 1898. Now it is illegal. It was a cruel sport, as the rabbits were on strange ground and did not have a chance to get away. Quite a lot of hare coursing was also done around here, and is still being run.

We have no sports now in the village at Christmas time — very different to what it was when I was a boy.

Now for my schooldays. I went to school when I was four. I do remember the first morning I went to school. I had a new sailor suit with a blouse, blue trousers and a hat with a shiny poke. I kept saying to myself "It's a *bought* suit, not a made suit." My older sister Millie took me. All the women in Hazells Lane where we lived came out and laughed to see us, and I remember going down the school path for the first time. I think the bigger children admired my new clothes.

There were no seats in my first classroom, but there was a gallery which ran the whole length. You got kicked in the back with someone's dirty shoes sitting up behind you. Sometimes someone fell from the top and came blundering down.

I was taught by the schoolmaster's wife until I was six or seven. We mostly sang hymns and learnt a few recitations. Then I went into Class One in the big room. We had iron seats with planks on them, and ink-wells with brass tops on chains (I believe I've got one in the Museum). If you slid along the plank to get out, you got a splinter in your backside.

We had Sunday School at school, not in the church. The teacher came back on Sunday and you had to go, even if you were Chapel people. The schoolmaster was the church organist. It was all church those days.

The name of the school is Filkins-cum-Broughton. It was built in about 1830. My father told me that when he first went to school they had to pay twopence per week. When I went to school we did not pay anything.

There were about a hundred children when I went, as they went to school then when they were four, and left when they were twelve. The schoolmaster taught in the big room with two helpers, and his wife taught in the classroom with one helper. Some of those helpers were children themselves, having barely left school — young girls who had not gone into service. In the School Log Book for 11th August 1900 there is an entry —

The lower standards are still restless and inattentive, and they contain some backward children. The strain of teaching and controlling such children ought not to be thrown on a girl of 14.

The bigger boys were appointed each week to light the fires in the winter and sweep up and dust the rooms. This meant an hour before school and an hour after, for which we received twopence a week. Children came from Langford Downs, Oxleaze, College Farm and Kencot Hill. They brought their dinner, but they had to eat it in the playground or out in the street, as they were not allowed in school except for lessons. There were quite big families from these outlying districts, and I can remember them coming down College Road with their little bags on their shoulders with what mother had made for them. It was usually a few slices of bread and lard with a sprinkling of sugar on it.

The school is about the same now as it was when I went to school, although they have new desks and better sanitary arrangements. I don't know what the teacher would do today if she had to pack a hundred children into the school.

The parson came down nearly every day to give us our scripture lesson. We had to learn the collect and a verse of a hymn. We got three marks on the register — one for attendance, one for the collect and one for the verse. These were counted up at the end of the year, and perhaps you got a prize. When we were old enough we had to go into the choir, which meant we had two services on Sunday and practice on Friday night. When we attended, it was marked on the register and we received a halfpenny, which was paid out at Christmas. If you misbehaved at any of the services, the parson would say "Swinford, you will be docked." This meant you lost your halfpenny, and if it occurred very often he would go and see our mother and tell her to give us a thrashing, which she obeyed. We had extra choir practice for Easter and Harvest Thanksgiving. There were big congregations at these services, every seat was full, and some had to stand around the font. We had a good choir then, all the choir stalls filled with men and boys, and seats in front for girls. Certain people had their own seats, and no one else was supposed to use them without permission. The sexton was very strict, and not particular about giving you a clout on the ear if you were talking or laughing. We always kept our eye on him.

Our school had its ups and downs. An entry in the School Log Book for 11th July 1899 reads —

Jesse Rowland here last evening, very abusive, firstly because the absences of his children had been reported, and secondly because his child had received a "hander" for swearing yesterday.

And on 20th February in the same year —

Mr and Mrs R. Carter sent to prison and the three children to the workhouse.

I started off fitting in well in the big room at school. I was interested in everything, but there was not a lot going on. I remember one of the recitations we learnt

King Bruce of Scotland flung himself down
In a lonely mood to think,
True, he was a monarch and wore a crown,
But his heart was beginning to sink.

The books were all about churches, it being a Church school. However, there was drawing, and I was a very good freehand drawer. The vicar used to give a shilling for the best drawing book every year for Standards 4, 5 and 6. When I got into Standard 4 I won it, but the shilling was never paid to me. The next year I should have had the Standard 5 book, but instead I had Standard 6. I won it then, but again I never had the shilling.

Now and then the magic lantern man used to come to our school. I remember his cork leg, which squeaked. We used to be naughty and throw our caps at the screen. The only slide I can remember had a man with a mouse running into his mouth. The lantern man had a carbide lamp, and the gas leaked into the gulley which ran under the school doorstep. One day I threw a match into it and it exploded, and cracked the step. You can still see the crack. I could never get on very well with the schoolmaster. He was from London, and he kept trying to take the mike out of us because we were country boys. One day he said to Sid Lewis: "What's the matter with thee?" "A wops stung I, Sir." "A *what*?" "A wops, Sir." "Spell it." "W-A-S-P, Sir." He had three sons and two daughters. Philip, his youngest son, was twelve months older than me, and he was put to take the class sometimes. He was not much good at marbles, and when I won he would say "Give I some", and I would say "No". Then he would kick up trouble, and I could not stand that so I'd tell him off. The next thing, he would tell the master I was refusing in class, and I would have to hold out my hand and get a good clout.

The school had no drinking water, and Philip had to fetch it from a well in the village. I would wait for him and catch him, and say "Now then, what about it?" and give him a good hiding. The road to the Post Office was paved, and the holes were filled in with gravel. Philip would throw it at us, and another boy and I threw it back. Presently, up came the schoolmaster with a lantern, and said he would fetch the police for throwing stones at his son. I ran away, but he caught the other boy, E. Willis, and we were summoned and had to go to court at Burford. We walked the five miles there and five miles back, and Mother had to pay the half-crown fine. She didn't know this would happen, but luckily she had brought a bit of money to buy us some dinner, so she handed this over, and we got something to eat from a relative in Burford.

The schoolmaster seemed to me to give me a thrashing for the least thing. If you had been out of school that morning, you knew you'd got to have it when you went back. So you put your old west-kits on, and two jackets on top. I remember going to school like that, and some men working on the Church Room laughed at me as I went past. One day I was given a thrashing which wasn't needed and when the master went to put the stick away in the desk, I ran up the school and opened the door. The children called "He's run, Sir!" I got my cap and away I went, up College Hill where some bigger boys were ploughing. I walked up and down with them until dinner time, and then I went to Mr Holloway, the blacksmith, and blew the bellows for him. He asked why I was not at school, and when I said "I runned off!" he told his wife. She came out with her apron full of apples with the bad bits cut off, and said "Now go back to school, won't you?" I managed to see my sister going back to dinner, and said "Don't tell Mother I runned out of school."

As I got older, I started to turn on the schoolmaster when he beat me, and kick his legs. Things went from bad to worse between us. An entry in the School Log Book for 5th June 1899, reads

> George Swinford continues his disobedient conduct and impudence, for which he has today been caned. His example was followed by Fred Flux, whose conduct has hitherto been good.

At last it got to a stand-up fight between us. All the girls started to scream and cry, and the boys shouted "Give it him, George!" In the afternoon I went down to school and he sent me back home. He had reported me to the school manager at Broughton Rectory, and he came and saw my mother, and ordered that my father was to give me a good hiding and I was to stand out in the room in front of all the school, and apologize to the schoolmaster.

I went down to school as usual on Monday morning, and the schoolmaster called me out into the room and said "Have you got anything to say?" I looked him straight in the face and said "No". He said I should go back home then. I went to school every morning and afternoon, and he would ask me again if I had any message, and when I told him "No", he would say "Well, go back home again". This I did for a month. The Education Authority wanted to know where I was, as I was marked absent. The schoolmaster told his story, but he did not tell the whole of it, so that when they came up to see my mother they were surprised to hear that I had reported for school every morning and afternoon, and had been sent back home.

It was discussed at a Board meeting at Witney, and it was suggested that I should go away to a relative to finish my schooling, but my father said "Filkins school for Filkins children", and he would not give way. The telegraph had just come to the village, and they couldn't get a boy, so I took on the job of taking round the telegrams. Then Miss Imms, the Post Mistress, was told she could not employ me, as I was meant to be at school. My sister Millie was thirteen and waiting to go into service, so she took the telegrams in school hours, and I did them the rest of the time. In the end, the School Manager asked me if I wanted to leave school and go to work and I said yes, and that is how I left school.

CHAPTER
THREE

Early Work and Marriage

My first job was nearby at Langford, gardening and leading some small children out in the donkey cart. I worked from 7 am till 7 pm, and got four shillings a week and a cup of tea and bread and butter with the girls, as they had servants. After six months I asked for a rise, but was refused. Then I was asked if I would take a job at Buscot Park in the stables, but I said "No, not horses". It would have meant staying away from home. and my mother did not want me to.

At the time Father was working at Shilton, and he asked me if I would like to come and work with him if he could get me a job, and I said I would. So that is when I started work on building and with stone, and I have never regretted it.

We worked at Shilton from 7 am till 6 pm five days, and Saturdays till 1 pm for which I got six shillings a week. When I first started I was not always sure I could do it, as it was three miles to walk there, and so cold. Sometimes I shed a few tears, and asked why could I not stay at home? When you got up in the morning your boots were so stiff you had a job to get them on. We were working for the church, walling. The walls were very dilapidated, and the gates had been neglected. It was winter-time, and we came to a pond which was frozen so hard that we could pile stones from the fallen wall on it. It was very awkward, getting round the pond to rebuild the wall behind it, so my father asked the vicar if he would pay a bit more for that part, but he said no. However, we managed to get a good few hares while we were on the job, and we took the old gateposts home as firewood for cooking them.

One day in 1900, before I was thirteen, we were at a cricket match and Mr Groves, the builder, was there. His firm was Alfred Groves and Sons, of Milton-under-Wychwood. He said "Is Jo Swinford here?" and Father said "I've got a son now. Any chance of a job for him?" and Mr Groves said "Yes, bring him along". So my father and I went to a quarry called Waterplain to chop stones for a potting-shed at Bradwell Grove, and we also repaired garden walls. We worked piece-work at one shilling and six pence per yard. This is how I started working for Mr Groves, and although there were some breaks when there was no work, altogether I was with him for twenty-five years, off and on.

My next job with Father was on a new house called Ravenshill at Botherop. It belonged to the man who owned Hatherop Castle nearby. We Filkins children used to sing

Southrop, Hatherop
Botherop and Eastleach
All begins with an A

In summer we worked twelve hours a day and six on Saturday. I got up at 3.45 in the morning and lit the fire and at 4 am Mother fried our eggs and bacon (we had our own hens then, about eighteen chickens generally). We started walking at 4.45 am as it took about one and a quarter hours. I had to mix the lime mortar — we did not have concrete then — and carry it up the ladder to the mason in a wooden hod with a long leg called a monkey. Sometimes I made the tea, but not very often as another labourer, who was not so strong and had bad feet and could not get up the ladder, usually made it. I also had to fetch two quarts of beer from The Victoria Arms at Eastleach for the foreman each day, and on Saturday morning I cleaned out the mess room.

We had an hour off at dinner-time, and one day I lay down in the long grass in the shade of a walnut tree and went to sleep, and I never woke till four o'clock and wondered where I was. Father was worried because I was not there to take his mortar, and everyone thought I might have fallen down the well. When he found me he gave two or three slaps on the head, but not hard. It was a long day, three miles each way to walk, which could take one and a half hours if you stopped for birds' nests or rabbits. If I was late the foreman stopped me a penny (I got twopence an hour), saying "Late again, you young beggar!" Often I had to sit down on a wall to get a rest on the way home, although I was a strong boy. After a time Father managed to get me a second-hand bicycle, which made it a great deal easier.

One afternoon the foreman said "It's time you started doing a bit of walling, George, so get a trowel and hammer and see how you go." Father got me a line, too, and that is how I started to handle stone as the men did (before that, I had been mostly fetching and carrying). I did well, and got a good recommendation from the foreman. Walling is not as easy as it looks. Years later I heard of a man watching a mason at work. He said he could not see that there was much in it, just putting one stone on top of another. The mason said "That's where you're wrong. It's putting one on top of two, and two on top of one."

In January 1901 we were finishing off a job doing the steps up to the front door. The bells started tolling in all the churches around — Eastleach Turville, Eastleach St Martin and Southrop — and the foreman said "The old lady's gone. I can see her now." We took off our caps and stood there until the bells stopped tolling. That was the end of our Queen Victoria whom we had known so long.

When my father and I went out for a whole day's work we took two meals — dinner and tea. Mother gave us each some potatoes and carrots to cook, in a bag, and we had our usual bit of bacon. I had a tremendous appetite, and one day I said "I feel like eating all mine for dinner." So Father, who always had a joke, said "Go on, then — I've got plenty." When it came to tea-time he got his out, and I had none. I watched him eating and said "You told me you had plenty." "So I have," he said, "plenty for myself." But of course he gave me some.

Next, Mr Groves sent us to Aldsworth, and as it was too far to walk we lodged there for the week. It was the first time I had been away from home. We stayed with a labourer who worked for William Garne, the brother of John Garne of Filkins, who I have mentioned. He too had a big flock of prize Cotswold sheep. It was very cold at night, and I remember how my father used to pick up the carpets and put them on the bed and then put them back on the floor in the morning, and he told me not to say anything about it. The first morning going to Aldsworth to work was very strange, setting off with a bag of tools and food for the week. The roads were too bad for cycling, so we had to walk. Father knew the short cuts across the footpaths, and I remember going up by Eastleach Downs across the old Bibury racecourse to Ladborough, and then on to Aldsworth.

When you stayed in lodgings you paid sixpence a week, and another sixpence for cooking the meat you brought, and if you wanted the farmworker's wife to supply and cook vegetables you paid an extra threepence.

The foreman, Reuben Timms, said "Have you done any walling?" and when I said yes, and I had my tools, he said "That's good, you can go and help your father." I was doing the same as the men by then as regards chopping and walling, and the foreman was pleased with me and told my father what a good boy I was. I was now getting threepence an hour.

When that work was finished, we were going on to a job at Burford Hospital, but it was put off for a while, and we had no work and no income. We spent the time working on our allotment, sawing up wood and doing jobs on our own house. We still had to pay the rates on the house, and for everything else, of course, but we got through. We had saved a pound or two when we were on long days, and Mother always managed to save a bit somehow. When I was earning well I gave Mother ten shillings a week, and she was pretty careful. I did any job that turned up, like putting a slate on a roof for two shillings. Father and Mother always paid up, although some did not. The farm labourers just *could* not. The baker would bring the bread to their door and say "Have you got any money now? I'm afraid I can't leave it, you owe so much," and then he would take the bread away.

Sometimes Mother would say "George, can you lend me a few shillings? I want to get some extra coal." She would also get some extra money off Father. Coal was eighteen shillings a ton, and generally they shot it off at your door, it being two shillings more if the horse and cart wheeled it round to the shed. Mr Garne, the farmer, had a big pile of coal up at Cross Tree for the thresher. People would come and steal it, of course, so he would get a man to splash lime all over it so that you could see where the hole was, and then he would go round and see who had coal spattered white.

In 1902 we got the job working on Burford Hospital, which included a lot of levelling and walling. My father was foreman. I remember the doctor (the one who had vaccinated my sisters) coming out and saying "You men — would you like a cup of tea?" He had a butler and footman, and tea, bread and butter and cakes were brought out, and he told us take home what we could not eat, which we did.

When I was sixteen I had my first pocket money, four

shillings a week. That is how I was able to lend Mother some money now and then. Before that, I gave all my earnings to her. As I said, when I was talking about my childhood, when we were boys we kept the odd pence we earned holding horses, fetching medicines, opening gates and so on, to spend on sweets or save for a new pocket-knife, but once I started work there was no more time for that.

In 1904 when I was seventeen we went to work on Eynsham Hall for Squire Mason, which was a big job. Work was not very brisk then. We were dressing stone, piece-work, so much a yard. We were six months there and six months in Witney.

In 1905 it was a terrible time, with no work anywhere. We rode hundreds of miles on our bicycles to try to get a job. So Father said, "What about Wales?" We started off with a good breakfast on a Monday, and rode from Eastleach, Cheltenham and Gloucester to Chepstow. We stayed the night there, and went round all the builders' yards, but there was nothing doing. We heard they were building docks at Newport, so we went there. The foreman said "What are you?" and Father said "Masons". He told us we had got there a fortnight too early, as they had no stone, and that we should come back later. We thought we would go on to Cardiff, but the men in the streets said not to, as there were hundreds out of work there. So we started to cycle home. We got to Cheltenham by midnight. and my front wheel got stuck in the tramlines and I fell off into a puddle of water which got into my acetylene lamp, so there was only a spark left. We passed a policeman leaning against a telegraph pole, and Father got dazzled when his lamp shone on the policeman's buttons, and he was so tired that he fell into the bank. The policeman said "You're drunk!" but Father lifted his fist and we rode off.

We got home early in the morning, and Mother woke up and got us our breakfast, and told us that Mr Willis, the Lechlade builder, would give us work. He was a relative of Mother's, as she was Belinda Willis before her marriage. We did odd jobs — chimneys on Railway Terrace (a row of old cottages) and work on the roof of Lechlade Manor. One day I was up a ladder working on a chimney when Sam Willis, the builder's son who was captain of the Lechlade Football Team, said "I want you to play for us." I said, "What's the fee?" and he said he would see to that, as he had seen me play.

By now, the Filkins Football Team had improved a great deal. A year earlier, on Good Friday, we had played against Lechlade, although on that occasion I did not play. My father and I were working in a quarry near Bimbury Lodge called Baker's Corner, chopping stones for a new wing on the Lodge. We were doing this piece-work, and my father said that if I were to work hard on Good Friday (which was a holiday) and do a lot, I could have the chance to ask Mr Groves for more money, as I was still having only threepence an hour. So I worked all day, and when Mr Groves measured up my work my father said "I should think the boy is worth a bit more money", and he said "Yes, I will give him another halfpenny an hour." So that is why I missed the match.

In 1907 we were out of work again. Then we heard

there was a big house being built at Furse Hill, Willersey, near Broadway. The road sloped down from the quarry, and the stone was dragged on a sledge by a horse. I remember one day when I was working a nightingale in a hedge nearby was singing fit to split the sky. I did a good job stone-dressing. The foreman was called Fox, and of course the men used to call "Tally-ho!" when he was coming. One day he said "Do you know anything about stone slating? I can't get a man who knows." I had worked a quarry and dug our own stones, as I told him, so he said he wanted me to go up and be in charge. So I agreed. I was now working on my own.

Then I had a winter's work at Fairford, which was a big thing. I helped to build two cottages on the Cirencester side near the river. While I was working at Sapperton I met Gimson, William Morris's pupil, who was designing buildings and furniture. I worked for him turning a coach-house and stables into garages. I also did some work for Gimson at his house. He had just bought a new motor car and I made him an inspection pit in the garage. Later, I put the wing on The Pig and Whistle at Quenington, and worked on pumps and windmills at Godwins opposite. A promised job at Bibury did not come off, and as I could not afford to hang about I packed my tools and left, along with my nephew. Next day was Michaelmas — I remember it as if it were yesterday. We took our bikes to Burford and Taynton, but they said "No work" so on to the Barringtons. No, they could not take us on there either. Then someone said "Tell you what — Mr Groves is building a couple of cottages at Sherborne." So we stopped at The Fox

Inn at Barrington and had two pennyworth of bread and cheese and a bottle of pop, and then off to Sherborne.

It was piece-work. It measures you up — an old game in those days. We started on a Tuesday. There were four more masons stone-chopping in the quarry. Saturday was kept in hand, as there was no work for us on Saturday or Monday — that is why we started on a Tuesday. However, we got more work done than the others who worked on Saturday and Monday as well. The foreman looked at my stones, which had to be stacked in cubic yards. He said nothing to me, but he said to the under-foreman "He's done all that in that time, better than our own men." The under-foreman did not like that. We got ourselves lodgings, and kept that job with Groves right up to 1914.

I worked four to five years at Burford, with up to twelve men under me. Father worked there too, but not on outside jobs. He was still with Groves when the War broke out. A lot of masons went into the timber yards, working with oak and ash, and some into Government jobs, building aerodromes. At Burford I worked on The Priory, Corner House, the rectory and the vicarage.

In 1912 we started rebuilding Filkins Hall, which had been burnt down in 1876. I remember the ruins very. well. In the cellars the foxes used to lay, and people with terriers got them out and shot them — of course this was done on the quiet. I shall be going into the history of Filkins Hall later. It had been bought to be rebuilt by a Colonel De Sales La Terriere, who engaged Mr Groves. On Easter Tuesday my father and I were sent to do a few jobs to the lodge so that the gardener could come and live there while he got the garden straight, and also acted as caretaker. While we were at lunch about 9.30 am my father said "Hark! I can hear Mr Groves coming. He's about early this morning." He used to ride a little motor bike, and you could hear him coming quite a long way off. But the sound got louder, and we said "What a funny noise he's making!" Then all at once over came an aeroplane just above the tree-tops. We could see the man sitting in it. That was the first aeroplane we ever saw. What a talk in Filkins that day!

We started cutting down the trees which had sprung up amongst the ruins which had fallen into the cellars, and then began to clear them out. I remember we found tons of lead amongst the stones and rubble, as the building had had a flat lead roof. We also found some clay pipes on a ledge under an arch, and also one bottle of champagne — the men soon had the top off that and drank it! When the Colonel heard he was annoyed, and told the men that if they found any more wine they should let him have it, and he would pay well for it. I do not think they found any more, but we did find a very nice iron fireback, weighing about a hundredweight, which is still in the fireplace in the hall. The date and initials were marked —

T E
1716

Lewis Jennings and his son Ivor were the foremen. I had the pleasure of laying the first stone for the new building, which was under the south front door. We worked long hours on the Hall — 6 am till 7 pm, with half an hour for breakfast and one hour for dinner. Wages for tradesmen were 6½d per hour — that was £1.14s.8d for a sixty-four hour week, working till one o'clock on Saturdays. Labourers' wages were 4d per hour, that was £1.1s.4d for the sixty-four hour week. We also had 6½d stopped for health and unemployment insurance. As the days got shorter we gradually worked shorter hours, until we got down to nine hours a day. In bad weather we had to lose time — if it rained we would stay in the mess room waiting for it to clear up so that we could put in a few hours. I have known times when we stayed on the job all day and never earned a penny. Men who came in and lodged in the village were allowed two shillings a week lodging money.

The old stone was used as far as possible. The only new stone was brought in for windows and doorways, which was worked on the job by the banker masons. By Christmas we had the building up, the roof on, and most of the windows fixed. This was the time when the Suffragettes were burning down places. Mr Groves was building a house in Somerset and during the weekend they burnt it down, and the Colonel, who had a house which was empty at the time at Cheltenham, had that burnt down, too, so during the Christmas holidays they asked me if I would be watchman at the Hall. So I spent Christmas from 5 pm to 7 am walking about on the premises, and received five shillings for each night. Later, we employed a man every night until Easter, and I relieved him when he wanted a night off.

The Colonel and his wife got into the house soon after Easter 1913, a year after we had started. Of course the men had to go off and find a job elsewhere. On Boxing

Day we had a strong west wind, and it uprooted some of the trees in the park, and in March a strong east wind uprooted some more. The Colonel was very much upset at seeing the old trees lying about on the ground and he asked was it possible to put some of them up again. He consulted Mr Groves and my father, and they agreed to try. My father and I and two men started to rear one back up, cutting the top off to about thirty or forty feet and digging a much bigger hole around the roots. We put packing under it, used screw jacks to raise it, and finally pulled it up with a winch. We replanted fifteen out of twenty-five trees, but only a few lived, as they were very old trees and all the large roots had broken off.

We found that when a tree falls it strikes back at the roots, and as some had blown down with a west wind and some with an east wind this made them out of line when we put them back up.

In 1914 when the War started I was building the Carter Institute. Mr J. Bowley was the contractor, and the stone came from Westwell Downs, on the right-hand side of the Barrington road. The money was left to build the Institute for the village by a Mrs Amelia Carter. I remember when I went to school this same lady used to give all the people in the village a tea-party. This was a noted day. I remember the lovely cake we had, and sweets and oranges, and how after the tea we had a concert with a string band from Lechlade.

While I was working on the Institute I was lent, along with my father and brother, to Mr Gimson, whom I have already mentioned, who was doing some work for William Morris's daughter May at Kelmscott. Gimson had designed a labourer's cottage to be built near the Manor House and he was building it with direct labour. Our family were his stonemasons. I did not think all that much of a job where there was not a proper building company, and the architect hired masons himself. May Morris was a pleasant woman, very like her father, always ready to support craft.

Afterwards I did several other jobs for Gimson. He had an architect pupil who was good at the job and we got on well together. We agreed that after the War, which had just started, that being 1914, we would carry on our partnership, but then he was called up, and six weeks later we heard that he had died at the front.

Now I must mention something about my family life. On Whit Monday, 5th June 1911, I was married to Ellen Susan Sowden at Lechlade church. Although I was a Methodist, I was married in the Church of England. The vicar hung about signing the certificate, as we were Chapel, but we got it in the end. Whit Thursday that year was Coronation Day for King George V, but as it was my honeymoon week I did not have much to do with the festivities. My wife was cook-housekeeper to a Miss Brownrigg, who rented a small farmhouse at Little Faringdon, called Common Farm, and ran a private school there. Miss Brownrigg gave us a very nice blue and white dinner service for a wedding present, which I still have on my dresser.

For the first six months of our marriage we lived at Kencot, until we could get a house in Filkins. Our house was opposite The Five Alls, and we lived there for fourteen years, that is, until 1926. My son George was born on 10th November 1912, and my daughter Freda in 1920. When I was first married and rebuilding Filkins Hall I was working fifteen hours a day. I worked on the allotment before I went to work in the morning, and again in the evening after I had finished at the Hall. In 1911 there were seventy-two or seventy-four (I do not remember for sure which) quarter-acre allotments up the Langford road opposite Filkins Mill. I was not able to get one for myself for some time, so Father who had two — that is, half an acre — let me use half of one of his for the time being.

We only had three and a half years of married life as a family, as the War came as an interruption. In 1915 I enlisted, and in 1916 I was called up.

CHAPTER
FOUR

Yesterday

Before I go onto the next part of my life, I shall go back and tell you about the village of Filkins as it was in my early days. I remember it as if it were yesterday.

Filkins is in the Bampton Hundred, Oxfordshire, and I have been reading a book called *The Place Names of Oxfordshire* by Margaret Gelling, based on material collected by Doris Mary Stenton. This is the record of the names of this village that have been found

Filching 1180. Filkinges 1185. Filking and Filkinch 1218. Fulking 1268. Filyking 1269. Filechinge 1285. Filekynges 1316. Fylkynche 1333. Fylkings 1347. Netherfilkynge 1360. Netherfilkynges 1383. Filkynges 1390. Fylkynge 1797. Over Filkins — Nether Filkins. Possibly the people of Filica but the forms are too late for any degree of certainty.

Our small river is called The Pills. In an old book of 1857 I have got there is a reference to a spring in this neighbourhood called Ewelme Pill, Ewelme meaning a river spring and Pill from Pyll, used in place names of a small stream. There is a large stone near the Cross

Tree which I have heard divided Filkins into two parts — Over Filkins and Nether Filkins. As Filkins was a hamlet of Broadwell, the name Filkins did not appear on the old maps.

I think the first thing to mention is stone, as the village is entirely built of stone. The floors, walls and roofs of our buildings are built from stone, fences, paths with crazy paving — even the footpaths in our village were paved, and when I was a boy I remember when they were taken up and broken for road mending. A few were left at the entrances to houses and cottages and are still there today.

The main street in Filkins is a portion of the road from Lechlade to Burford. The part from the Bakehouse to The Lamb Inn in front of the church is a new piece built since the church was built, and the village green went up to the wall now enclosing the Bakehouse field. The old people called it the New Road. The main road used to pass in front of the old vicarage and up the back of the church to The Lamb Inn. The main street has some dangerous bends, which is rather a nuisance these days for the modern traffic.

The lanes are named Hazells Lane after G. Hazell, the shoemaker, who lived there when I was a boy, and Rouse's Lane after a family who lived there. Then there is Kemps Lane, this name is not used much now, but the old people used to call it Kemps Lane as a Mr Kemp lived in an old cottage at the entrance to St Peter's House, and from there to my house is Kemps Lane. Lamb Lane is from The Lamb Inn to the cross roads going to Langford, and Cross Tree Lane is from the Cross Tree to the cottage at the back of the farm buildings. Rags Lane is now from the Kencot road to the back of The Bull Inn.

The old people used to talk of Filkins as if it was a town. They used to say "the allotments at the top of the town". "Up behind the town" was up the Kencot road. We have three bridges in the village. The present Broughton Bridge is the third one I can remember built there. The first old bridge with two stone arches was pulled down and rebuilt with black brick stones when I went to school, then in 1925 that was pulled down and rebuilt with one concrete arch. Sher Bridge is on the Langford road, and is still the old stone arch. Town Pool Bridge near Goodfellows is a very old bridge with two stone arches and a square drock. There was also a ford where traps or carts used to drive through to cool the horses' legs and also for them to have a drink. A notice board at these old bridges read thus, "These bridges are insufficient to carry weights beyond the ordinary traffic." Signed J. Powell, Surveyor.

A lot of old cottages have been pulled down since I can remember, and of course some have been built, also some farm buildings which were in bad repair have been taken down, but we still have old buildings left in the village now. A datestone on the Bakehouse occupied by Mr J. Clark can be seen.

```
        T
T            A
     1626
```

This place is very interesting as there is a tunnel running from the house into a deep pond at the far end of the orchard, where you can still see the arch. Mr Clark's father went up the tunnel some distance, but found it had fallen in. The tunnel was used, they say, at the time of the Civil Wars as an escape route. A small boat was in the pond at the outlet of the tunnel, where the escaping man rowed himself across and went up some steps and got away, leaving the man who was chasing him with the deep pond in front of him and no boat. Nobody seems to know where the entrance is, but it is not needed now. I expect it was filled in.

The heap of earth by the side of the pond from where it was dug, about twenty feet high, is called the Mounty Bank. The family of Clark have lived here for a long time — I remember three generations.

Another old house which used to be the Brewery stands at the north end of the village towards Burford. I do not remember any brewing done there, but I do remember the buildings (now pulled down) where the windows were made of lattice work to let out the steam. A Mrs Clark lived there when I was a boy, and she had horses and carts and did hauling, and was also our village coal merchant. They hauled one ton of coal and shot it up by your house for eighteen shillings. The date on the house is 1688, and there is also an old sundial on the house. This house is now Pear Tree Farmhouse, but the house opposite used to be Pear Tree Farm when I was a boy, owned by the family of Pryor. The two cottages at Gassons View have mullioned windows, and are dated at about 1714. The buildings at the back have large stones on the roofs. One I have measured is seven feet six inches by six feet. These cottages and buildings were occupied by a family named Farmer, who were masons. I shall be writing more about them in another chapter. At the corner of Rouse's Lane, next to Gassons View, is a cottage now called Vine Cottage. It is fenced with great stones called planks, which I shall write of later. This used to belong to Jesse Farmer and his sister who kept the shop where we bought our sweets. At the corner of the lane Donkey John Farmer once kept his cart, and the donkey was kept in what is now the end part of the Museum. Later Jesse Farmer kept his horse and cart there.

The row of cottages near Town Pool Bridge were once a malthouse. The house where I now live was the maltster's cottage until about 1800. Pieces of red malting tiles can still be seen in the walls. In 1931 we made three cottages from the five old ones. Opposite it was The Smithy, where the horses were shod by Mr F. Trinder when I was a boy.

I have heard that the Old Vicarage was built for a hotel, but was never used as such. It was to be named The Green Dragon. It was taken over for use as a vicarage when the church was built, then in 1935 it was sold, and has changed hands several times since then. Auburn Cottage is the only brick-built cottage in the village, and I think it is an eyesore to everybody. It was built by a man named Clack in 1870. He went to America in his youth and saved a bit of money, and came back and built it. He was called America Clack. When he died, his widow lived there for some years. I have already mentioned her as Granny Clack, the old lady I used to go and talk to when I was a little boy. Towards the end of her life she became very funny, and said the Devil was up her chimney. Harry Robey asked her if he should come and shoot him, and she said she would be pleased if he would, so he took his gun and shot up the chimney, knocking down buckets of soot. The old lady said she never heard anything of the Devil after that, and was quite happy.

There have been several shops in the village. Opposite the barn at Broughton Bridge is the large general shop I have already mentioned. Old Mark Cook used to say a piece of poetry about it, but I can only think of the first verse, which went like this —

> When you stand on Broughton Bridge
> It will sure to make you stare
> To see a grand and noble shop
> And all the nice things there.

The datestone on the row of cottages adjoining reads —

R	O
1833	

Only one is occupied now, and they will be taken down when empty. The first shopkeeper I remember was Richard Gardener. I have already mentioned the little shop at the end of Rouse's Lane kept by Jeannette Farmer, where we got our sweets. Then next to Filkins Farm there was another shop. The datestone reads —

	G
H	N
1746	

I remember when it was the Post Office. A man named Piggott lived there, and on the wall was a fire insurance plaque.

The history of Filkins Post Office is interesting. When I was a little boy in 1890 the postman walked from Lechlade to Kelmscott, then to Langford and then to Filkins. He had lost an arm and had a wooden one with a hook on it to pick up the bag. A jokey sort of fellow — he would catch at your legs with his hook. At that time the Post Office was run by Piggott. Then it moved to Holloway's, the blacksmith, and Miss Holloway ran it. We found the first post box under the bow window. The telegram service came in in 1900, and I took the telegrams round out of school hours, as I said earlier. Then the Post Office went to The Bull Inn, which had closed down, and Mrs Imms and then Mr Isaacs ran it. Then it came back to where it is now, next to Filkins Farm. There was always a shop with it. At one time a collie dog carried the parcels and letters strapped onto his back. I have the collar with his name and address engraved in brass in the Museum. I used to walk round with him sometime to lone places like Grafton.

The date on the house where Mr Holloway the blacksmith worked is 1812. It is next to the Museum, which I shall write about later. Before Mr Holloway, a man named Cockbill ran a blacksmith's and wheel-wright's shop. He was also the undertaker, and in the old parish book it says: "Paid Mr Cockbill for coffin 10s, shroud 1s.6d., and 3s.6d. for beer at the funeral." I remember the old sawpit being filled in, where they cut out the coffin boards from elm trees. As I said, Mr

Holloway took over the business. He was a clever man. He made the altar rail in the church, the grapes being made from horseshoe nails. When bicycles came in he started a cycle shop, repairing, and letting out bicycles at sixpence an hour.

In Filkins we had four inns, The Bull, The Lamb, The Five Alls and The Fox. The Bull was closed during the First World War, about 1917, and after that it was used, as I have said, as the Post Office. It is a very old building, and a lot of drinking went on there. When we were boys we would wait outside to see the men fall down the steps as they came out. One of the most well-known customers was Mr Thatcher, a horse-dealer. My father told me some stories about him. When he was drunk he would fall from his trap, and he broke both arms and both legs at different times. He was a wonderful man with horses. I have heard say that if anyone sold him a horse that had been faked, he would fake him up and sell him back to the same man for more money than he gave for him, then he would tell the man. If anyone wanted a pony they would send to him and ask him if he had one of a certain size, etc. He would then get all his horses together, and ask the young men of the village to help him take them out. Each man rode one and drove another.

My father told me how they went to Lechlade once and sold one horse for a good price. Thatcher was very pleased about this and of course it meant having some beer on the deal, and some of them had more than they should. They arrived back to Filkins at different times, and late at night one man and his horse were still missing, so they got their lanterns and went out in different directions to find him. They could hear a horse coming up the Langford road, so they waited. It was the missing man and horse, the man firm asleep with his arms round the horse's neck, and the horse gently making his way home. The man's name was George Giles.

Mr Thatcher was also a noted poacher. He always kept some good dogs, and they used to lay in the bed of his trap. If he saw a hare in a field as he was going round the countryside he would send them after it. He had one large greyhound which would catch a hare, bring it back and jump up into the trap with it. But Thatcher was caught a good many times, and had to pay for his sport. When he was summonsed for poaching and went to Burford Police Court, they asked him if he was guilty or not guilty. He replied, "Never mind about that, what have I got to pay? Whether I be guilty or not, I know I shall have to pay, so don't let us waste any more time."

At The Lamb Inn they used to brew their own beer and ever since I can remember the large vat was over the room near the back door, and the copper furnace on the ground floor where they boiled the beer. The first landlord I remember was Alf Spiers. I shall be writing more about him when I go into the history of football in Filkins. There is also a club room there, where the Red, White and Blue Club had their headquarters, and I shall say more about this, too, later.

The name The Five Alls sounds rather peculiar to some people. The meaning is — The Parson prays for All, the Farmer sows for All, the Soldier fights for All, the Lawyer pleads for All, and the King rules for All. The main house dates from about 1700. I remember a row of coach-houses and stables being pulled down. When I was a boy a man named Burrows used to come and stay for about a month. He was agent for Brades, the cutlers, from Sheffield. He had a large covered waggon where he kept his cutlery, and every day he would be off with two big black horses around the countryside, selling his wares. In the evening he would lay out his goods on the village green for the villagers to buy a pocket knife, a hoe, a billhook or some other tool they needed. His tools were noted as good, and if we boys had one of Burrows's pocket knives, we thought a lot of it. If you did get a bad tool he would exchange it for a new one next time he came. He used to stay here for a month in the spring and a month in the autumn. When he first arrived he would spread out his wares near The Lamb, and we boys received a few coppers for going round the village with a bell, telling them Mr Burrows was come again. Later, he was getting on in years, and after an illness he settled down and made his home at The Five Alls until he died. His old waggon fell to pieces in the yard, and his old horses died before he did. I remember one's name was Dumplin. I still have one of Burrows's axes.

Opposite The Five Alls was another inn called The Fox. You can still see the name on the wall in black paint — F.O.X. It was closed before I can remember, and Mr W. Trinder bought it and used it as a builder's yard. He was our village undertaker, wheelwright and general builder. I remember his men sawing up trees on the sawpit for coffin boards, and for repairs to waggons, carts, etc. I do not think he built new waggons or carts, but there were always a lot of these lying about the yard to be repaired. He also made wheels, and I remember him running them up the street to be bonded by the blacksmith. He made the village bier, which was in use for many years. Mr Trinder died in 1926. One of his two sons, Kenneth, was killed in the 1914–18 war. There are two date stones on the house, as shown below. One is on the gable, and one on the quoin. I think the house was built at two different times, as you can see that the walling is different. At one time Mr Robbins ran a cycle business there.

We have two mills in Filkins. The mill near the bridge between Filkins and Broughton Poggs is very old, built in 1580. It has done good service, but now the mill is silent and the water-wheel is falling to pieces. The barn near the bridge, dated 1883, used to belong to the mill, where they stored corn for grinding. It was lent to the parish for storing and thrashing. I remember seeing men there in winter in overcoats, thrashing with a flail. The other mill is on the Langford road. The mill is old, but the house has been built since, in about 1880, from stone used from the ruins of Filkins Hall after it was burnt down in 1876. You can still see the red burnt stone in the walls. This mill is still used for grinding, but not so much as it used to be, for I remember when a miller and a carter were employed. My mother used to have the wheat which we had leased during the harvest ground into flour. The miller kept the bran and toppins to pay for the grinding, and Mother made bread and cake from the flour in the old cottage oven twice a week.

There were, of course, many farms in the village and nearby, but there is so much to say about them, and about agricultural work and the men who did it that I shall leave this for the end of this chapter, and go on to the Workhouse. This was at Cross Tree. There were two cottages, which have since been turned into one. As you entered the front door you turned right for men and left for women. Downstairs each had one large room, and upstairs it was the same, with a large attic for each, with no partitions in those bedrooms. On the women's side there were also wash-houses. Of course each part had its own staircase, and its own back door. Women who were unable to go out to work did weaving and the washing, while the men cut up wood and did other odd jobs in the barn adjoining. There was a great deal of poverty. Some old people were looked after by their sons and daughters, but any trouble and they would say "We'll send you to the Workhouse". There were two Coal Charities, one started in 1700, which helped a bit. They were for the old people, but sometimes the parson decided who was old. It was a problem for people keeping warm. You would go to a piece of ground called Furzey, which belonged to the village, to draw a faggot to hot your oven, but it was in the middle of Squire Fox's land, and interfered with his hunting.

One old chap, Bert Taylor, who was not all that sharp-like, ran away from the Workhouse. I asked him why he did not like it there, and he told me you have to be careful, as if you refused to take your medicine "They gets you down on the bed and holds your nose and pours it down your throat, and very likely you're a corpse in the morning." Fortunately a certain woman in the village took him in and looked after him till he died. Bungy, we used to call him.

I have an old parish book dated 1796–1823, where the Workhouse is mentioned very often. To quote some entries —

1803   Paid William Purbrick rent of the Workhouse £20.

1804   Paid Cooper Clinch for two tubs and one bucket for use of the Workhouse £1.

            Paid William Carter for eating and liquors at the meeting for letting the Workhouse £5.12s.10d.

            Paid Thomas Adams day's work for cutting chaff for the Workhouse beds.

The Pest House, as it was called, was situated in the field between the Pills and the Eastleach road, about a hundred yards from the road. This has now been pulled down, and the stone used for repairing the farm buildings at Peacock Farm. I had pointed out to me the stones in the walls which came from the Pest House.

Entries in the parish book concerning the Pest or Smallpox House —

Paid Sam and Porter a bill for wood, bacon and other food for the smallpox folk in my house up in the field £3.0s.10½d.

Paid Joseph Carter for necessitys for Sarah Clack's family when had the smallpox £1.12s.9d.

Paid for milk and mutton for the smallpox folk £1.0s.2d.

It was not until 1857 that we got a church of our own in Filkins. Before that you had to get christened, married and buried at Broadwell. There was a footpath across the big common, the first part was the Gravel Walk. There were special stiles to rest the coffin on. You had six men — "four a-carrying, two a-resting". You paid eight shillings for beer at the burial, and ten shillings for the coffin. That was for the poor people. If you could afford it you had a pony and trap. Filkins people were buried at this end of the churchyard, towards Filkins, and you can see so-and-so of Filkins written on a lot of the gravestones.

Our church was built on the land which was the village green. The wall stone came from Kencot Hill and was given by Squire Harvey, who lived at Bradwell Grove. The Smith family who lived at Filkins Hall did a great deal towards raising funds for the building of the church. I have heard the old people say that the Smiths offered to give a peal of bells if they would build the church in the field opposite, which now belongs to the Bakehouse. What a pity this offer was not accepted. The freestone came from Windrush where they used to mine the stone, and the Windrush masons, who were called Jackson, also were the builders of the church. A pity red tiles were used for the roof in a village where there are plenty of stone tiles for the digging of them. The west gable is very good, and the pillars and arches inside, too.

Mrs Boulter, who was Robert Swinford's sister, told

me she remembered when the church was opened, as all the schoolchildren marched round it singing hymns. I have a plan of the church when the vestry was enlarged. This was done by R. Farmer, but I am not sure of the date. On the plan is written —

A grant of £90 towards the erection of this church was made by the Incorporated Society for promoting the enlargement, building and repairing of churches and chapels on the express and acknowledged condition that seats should be reserved for the use of the poorer inhabitants of this parish for ever, such seats being distinguished by the numbers 13, 14, 21 to 51.

These seats are numbered on the plan I have, also the pulpit is shown on the opposite side from where it now stands, and there is no organ marked on the plan. The vestry at the back of the church has not been done many years. I remember when Mr W. Trinder did it. The black and white marble tiles in the chancel were given by Sir Stafford Cripps, and A. Simpson, H. Puffitt and myself put them down. The window in memory of Lady Weaver I also fixed for her husband, Sir Lawrence Weaver. In Thomas Banting's history of Filkins (which I shall quote from later) he says that one Jane Hilby, whose husband was for many years shepherd for Mr Large of Broadwell, was the first person to be buried in Filkins churchyard. In the church hangs a board with the names of all the vicars of Filkins from 1864. I cut these names out in about 1952 for Dr Ede. The church has two bells. When we were children we used to say that the bells said "Who'll help — we two, we two", and the Broughton church with only one bell said "I, I."

The cemetery was given to the village by Captain Campbell, the owner of Filkins Estate. Soon after the 1914–18 War the vicar called a parish meeting to discuss arrangements for a cemetery. He took the chair and told everyone that the meeting had been called to decide how to get funds for putting up fences. When asked if we had got a cemetery, he replied yes, Captain Campbell had given the parish a portion of the little field at the back of the village, and the vicar and churchwardens had been appointed trustees. This caused a storm. A lot of people walked out of the room, while others stayed and argued against the way this affair had been kept from the village until money was wanted, and some people would not subscribe.

In his history, Thomas Banting mentions the birth of Baptists in Filkins. This is some of what he had to say —

At somewhere about the time of my birth, 1814, the Baptists came and introduced themselves into the village of Filkins. I remember an incident which happened at a house which stood where the Lamb Inn stands now. At that time there was a cottage and garden with a hedge round, and a window faced the street. While there was a prayer meeting being held a lot of young lads got up a row and throwed stones in at the window and struck several persons. A Mr Clark preached there at the time, and he took out a warrant against two of them although the Magistrates was very reluctant to grant it, as the dissenters at that time was in very bad odour. But they were committed for trial at the following assizes when a young man named William Adams went as a witness for them. The council for the prosecution says to him, I suppose you hallowed and flung the same as the rest. Oh yes, he says. Just stand down here along with the other two. So he got tried on his own evidence and they all had to pay £25 fine each or remain in prison until they could. The primitive methodists did not come here for about 15 or 16 years afterwards. A man by the name of Alcock was the first, he came and preached out in the street, they met with great opposition from uproar and addled eggs being thrown at them. Now there is a chapel for each denomination.

Mr Charles Farmer has written the history of Nonconformity in Filkins. This is some of what he wrote —

It appears that the Baptists were the first to hold meetings or services in Filkins. On a tablet in Cote Chapel there is the name of the (minister) that missioned Filkins. Why he chose to evangelize Filkins from other villages I cannot say, perhaps it had a bad repute . . . He began holding open air services, but encountered much opposition and persecution . . . There appeared to be ring-leaders which made others worse. Often he had to endure heckling and shouting . . . But not every one opposed, for we hear that the Landlord of the Lamb Inn loaned him a room in which to hold the service.

One night the roughs caught a lot of wild birds

alive, and the window being open they let the birds into the lighted room. They flew about knocking over candles and turning the room into darkness and chaos . . . Three or four of the men were summonsed to appear before the magistrates . . . When the case was on, two of the magistrates were inclined to ridicule the whole affair, and even said the men had as much right as the minister had to preach . . . (However) at least one of them said a serious offence should get a serious fine, so . . . they were fined £10 each or six months' imprisonment . . . Their wives travelled many miles round the countryside asking for help . . . At last the fines were paid and the men set free. It was said that two of the men became supporters of that which before they had persecuted. One of my relations then lived in the house known as Gassons View, and it is said they were some of his best friends, and often gave him encouragement and refreshment.

There were better times in store, for soon after a Chapel was built. My father often talked of attending services there with a Mr Clark, Landlord of the Fox Inn, and helped find the hymns. The Chapel was well built, and had a large lead tank inside for adult baptism . . . The Chapel is now closed and used as a garage, it stands not far from Broughton Bridge on the Kencot road, and is occupied by Mr Harris who keeps the shop close by.

The Methodists came upon the scene rather suddenly about 1834. My grandfather and his brother had been to Broadwell to spend the evening . . . On nearing home, they heard singing on the green near the Bull Inn, and there stood a little company of people holding a service. My Grandfather said I like their singing and the note of certainty. They heard of things they knew nothing about... I often wish I knew the names of those young people who came to Filkins. We made up our minds to throw in our lot with them that night, and from that simple yet beautiful service a society was formed which has continued to this day. It was plain they would soon meet with persecution, but not so severe as the Baptists. Services were held in cottages and open air. It seemed impossible to get a site on which to build till at last a small plot of land was bought which is now part of the Museum. In the years 1847–48 things were going very well. It was said that Broadwell people came to Filkins to Chapel, and Filkins people went to Broadwell to Church.

There are many more interesting things Charles Farmer wrote about the early Methodists. I will quote one more piece —

About 1895 a few members decided to form a brass band. This caused a sensation in the village. It was called Filkins Temperance Band, and this grew from four or five members to a very good band of fifteen players. About 1900 it was called Filkins Primitive Methodist Band, and it played at all the (open-air) camp meetings. The first Sunday out was on Whit Sunday, the Chapel anniversary. The players met at the Cross Tree and played a few tunes, then marched down to the bridge and back to the Chapel by 2.30. After a service they marched to the Cross Tree again.

There were several members from Langford and other villages around, and these players were invited to tea with other members. After tea they met again at the Cross Tree, and again played down to the bridge and back again for the service at 6.0 pm. After the service the band was out somewhere every Sunday until the autumn. (It) was steadily improving, and used to draw a large crowd, and was asked to attend flower shows and garden parties. This did not please all the members, and a few harsh words were said when they started to play dance music. Mr John Farmer and his four sons were the main stay of the band at that time.

The principal work of the village was agriculture. I shall mention seven farms, starting with those furthest out of the village. Filkins Downs Farm is about one and a half miles from the village and consists of a farmhouse and three cottages. The farmhouse is a good building, and there are some good barns and other sheds. The three cottages are built of stone — one is called Moneys Lodge. The farm is on the right of the Barrington road and now belongs to Bradwell Grove estate. College Farm is also on the right of the Barrington road, about a mile from the village, and it also belongs to the Bradwell Grove estate. There are some beautiful barns there with hipped roofs, and the farmhouse is very well built. There are three cottages, one near the house and two on the left of the Barrington road. Furzey Hall Farm is about one mile from the village on the left of the Burford road. There is a nice old stone barn there, but the house is not a very good building, I think. I have heard old men say that in the past, before my time, the farm was not cultivated well. My father said that a man who lived there once went to plough with a cow and a horse together. This farm too belongs to the Bradwell Grove estate.

Now for the farms in Filkins itself. Goodfellows Farm was called Moat Farm when I was a boy. I shall be writing about the burning down of the house and rebuilding of it later. A man called Glover farmed there until 1900, then a Captain Wahab. In 1920 it was sold to Sir Stafford Cripps. It was always considered a good sheep farm.

Pear Tree Farm up at Cross Tree belonged to the Pryor family who lived there for nearly a hundred years. The father left it to his three sons who carried on until they died. Then it was sold to Mr Goodenough of Filkins Hall and became part of his estate.

Peacock Farm was about fifty acres, the land running from Town Pool Bridge to the Pills, the datestone on the house is Jonah Basset 1730. Later it was sold to Dr Moore who had retired, and I cut out his and his wife's initials on the quoin, F.W.M. and W.M. 1936–53. This house is supposed to be haunted, and the old people say hammering could be heard at night. When I was a boy it belonged to Mr Hiett who also had Oxleaze Farm at Southrop. He ran the two farms together. He used to work oxen on the farm, and we boys used to ride back on the empty wagons. At Town Pool there was a ford through the brook, and the oxen would walk over the bridge with a load of corn, but going back empty they would always walk through the ford to have a drink and a splash. If we tried to make them go back over the bridge they would stand still until we let them go through the water and have their drink, then when they had had a rest they would start off to fetch another load. The farm buildings are now used by my brother as a builder's yard. There are two or three barns, and one was a large pigeon house years ago.

Mr John Garne (born 1821) came to Filkins in 1851 and took over what was then called The Manor Farm, and later Filkins Farm. The farmhouse was being restored at the time, and he lived in the house opposite the rickyard while it was got ready for him. I have heard that the Colstons built the farmhouse and the large barn at Cross Tree, which is twenty-two yards long and seven yards wide, its date stone being 1720. John Garne bred a fine flock of true Cotswold sheep, and he was very interested in Shorthorn cattle. He received many prizes for both. He had three sons and one daughter, John, Robert, William and Jane, of whom none got married. William worked on the farm from the age of seven. We boys used to ride on the huge rams, and we caught a lot of rabbits on the farm, as William was always in one of the pubs and we knew his habits.

Jane always lived at home, she was very heavy, weighing about twenty stone, and the groom and gardener had to get her out of bed.

John Garne was reckoned to be a good farmer and was liked in the village. Although he had a dominating way and used to shout and swear a lot he had some good points, for if anyone went to the farm with a message or some goods there was always food and beer or cider. He did not like parting with money, but he was good to the poor, and was a churchwarden. He drove a gig, and when he got older he had a low four-wheeler which was easier to get into. I remember him as an old man with two sticks and a stove-pipe hat. They called him Dada Garne then.

The labourer's wages when I first remember were ten shillings a week and cottage, the shepherd, cowman and carter three shillings extra. John Garne used to pay the men on Saturday night from 5 pm to 8 pm. I remember seeing the men's wives standing with the babies by the little shop at the gate waiting for their husbands to come out, so that they could go to the shop and buy groceries for the week, and if the man had some of his pay docked the wife would cry. Some of those families had six or eight children, and they did not get any luxuries in those days.

John Garne's yard up at Cross Tree was a very busy place. The cowsheds were built in 1850 and three men milked thirty or more cows, there were also pens of calves and store cattle. He had four two-horse teams and other horses which were being broken to harness, with several busy carters. There were sheds for donkeys and for their carts in which the shepherds took hurdles up onto the Downs to the sheep. In 1908 after John Garne had left, which was in 1900, the donkey shed, chaff house, wheat barn and ricks were taken away and a dutch barn put in instead. The cows and cattle went in 1960, and after that the new by-pass road cut off the yard from the farmland.

Mr Garne's cottages for farm labourers up at Cross Tree were very bad slums, as I have said. They made butter and cheese at the farmhouse, I remember fetching salt butter at one shilling a pound. They also made their own cider, I remember the cider mill in the yard by the back door and the horse going round and round. In 1887 when Filkins Hall was burnt down Mr Garne stood near the horse-drawn fire engine and gave the men the time by shouting Pump! Pump! He was always called Pump Garne after that. When the old man died his son John (Jackie) took over the farm and looked after it very well for a few years, then he took to drink and they all died middle-aged people. Jackie was a very fast driver in his gig, and known for his shouting.

Mr N. Hoddinott took over the tenancy of the farm in 1902 until 1929, then he left it in the hands of his oldest son. Two years later a Mr Saunders came and farmed it until 1939, then Mr Arkell was farmer until 1943. Now Mr John Cripps is doing it with Mr Jim Farmer, as it belongs to Mr Cripps. I helped restore the stables and coach house in 1930, a year after Sir Stafford Cripps bought it. I remember that Sir Stafford was not very satisfied when Mr Saunders farmed for him, as they threw everything out of the window into the garden.

Farm labourers worked long and hard days. The men in charge of the livestock worked and lived with them twelve or fifteen hours a day, feeding and caring for them all the year round, Sundays included. The carter would get his horses into the stable by 5 am and give them their feed, then he would go back home and have his own breakfast, then back to the stable about 6.30 am, and with the under-carters the horses were got ready and harnessed for work by 7 am, then out to the fields to plough, etc. At 9 am they had a break for lunch, about fifteen minutes, then at 12 pm about half an hour for dinner, when the horses' nosebags were put on. They worked on until 3.30pm, and then they shut off, as they called it, and went home. The horses were fed, and then the carter went home for his tea while the under-carters cleaned the horses, and cleaned out the stable. The under-carters generally finished about 5 pm, but the carter came back and gave the horses more food, until about 7 pm, when the horses were turned into a yard in the winter or a field in the summer. I have often wondered how many miles they walked up and down the fields every day, but they seemed happy. One could hear the boys singing and whistling as they went, especially after they had been to Burford Fair and heard some new tunes on the organs of the roundabouts. What a difference today — instead of whistling and singing you hear the roar of the tractors.

The cowmen had to get their cows in by 6 am, do the milking, then go home to breakfast, come back and clean out the cowsheds and get the food ready for the cows when they came in at 3 pm to be milked again. This was all done by hand and of course the calves had to be fed and looked after, which meant work to be done after tea. The shepherd's worst days were in the lambing season. He had a hut near the lambing pen where he slept and lived to be close at hand. Sometimes the worst weather throughout the winter was in January and February, but the shepherds seemed to like the work and did it for a good many years. In June there was the sheep-shearing, which the shepherds did by hand.

The general labourers who did jobs such as hedge-cutting, thatching, mowing and haymaking, etc. were called day men. They were expected to do any job on the farm, and they worked from 7 am till 5 pm for six days of the week. They did a lot of piece-work, hoeing and mowing by the acre, and hedgecutting by the chain. This gave them a chance to earn a bit of extra money by working longer days. Years ago farm work was looked upon as an unimportant job, with very low pay and bad housing conditions. I am glad to say that now things have altered, and they call the men farm workers instead of the old word, labourers, and since we have had two major wars we have all realized how vital farm workers and the land they cultivate is to this island of ours. We must not forget the women who helped to do some of the work on the land. When I was a boy every farmer employed some women, winter and summer.

It sounds strange to say that men went from Filkins to London to do haymaking, but it was so. I have known of six to eight men who used to go every year. Some of them walked and others who had the money to pay the fare went by train. They mowed the parks and fields with the scythe, then helped to make the hay and put it into ricks. At this time all traffic was horse-drawn, and hay was an important item for those who had horses to keep. The mowers slept in sheds and cooked their own meals, and did most of the mowing by contract. I have heard them say that they were up in the morning by 4 am whilst the dew was on the grass, then they would have a sleep at midday when the sun was hot, then work on until dark. They earned good wages like this, and could send money back to their wives, and when they came home they had a bit to bring with them. Of course some of the mowers did not benefit, as it was a drinking job until they had spent out, but I suppose they had a holiday. One thing I always remember is the clay pipes they brought home with them. All the smokers in the village were smoking London clay pipes after the mowers got back.

I remember the last year they went, which was about 1912. The men who went were Bert Cook, Sam Cook, George Cook and old Willoughby Adams. It was a sad ending to London haymaking. One of the mowers caught a hare in a snare, and as I said they cooked their own food. So of course they cooked the hare in a tin drum and let it stay there for some time, and then when they felt like it they went and had some. They were all taken ill the next day, and had to go to hospital. They had food poisoning and poor old Willoughby Adams died. The others came back home, and one by one they got better, but it was a long time before they could start work again. I have heard the old men talk of the time they used to go up to London haymaking, and when the work was done they worked their way back by doing hoeing for the market gardeners. After working a week in one place they walked on Sunday a few miles nearer home, and by the time they got to Wantage the harvesting was ready, as it was earlier on the Downs than it was here. Those were the days when they cut it by hand with a fagging hook. They arranged it so that they got back to Filkins by the time the harvest was ready here. When they had finished here they could go on as far as Northleach, where the harvest was later still. Some of these men who were careful with their money saved enough to keep them through the winter, with a few days thrashing now and then, and a bit of poaching with a dog and a gun and a few snares. Of course this happened before I can remember.

CHAPTER
FIVE

The Day Before
Yesterday

I have no records of who built the first Filkins Hall or when, but the Colston family were there from the middle of the eighteenth century until 1828. They were descendants of Edward Colston, who died in 1721. I have an engraving of him, dated 1722, and on the bottom is written

Edward Colston Esq, the brightest example of Christian liberality that this age has produced, both for the extensiveness of his charities and the prudent regulation of them. In whose Hospital, School and Almshouses, erected and fitted up at Bristol at ye expence of many thousand of pounds and endowed with a very plentiful estate, 106 boys are for ever clothed, maintained, educated and usefully placed out, 40 more clothed and qualified for businesse by a thorough instruction in writing and Arithmetic and 30 more men and women harboured and competently supported for life. From whom many Charity schools in several parts of England had large donations. Most of the churches in Bristol and some elsewhere obtained great sums towards their rebuilding, repairing and beautifying. All ye hospitals and Workhouses in London and Bristol, and the societys for Propagating the Gospel received very large benefactions and 80 poor livings a considerable Augmentation by whom sufficient provision in many places was made for ever, for prayers, Sermons and Catechetical Lectures and many other Charities bestowed not here mentioned, besides his private ones probably not inferior to those known which will then first be made publick when they meet with their reward.

J. Richardson, P. C. Vertue Sculptor

This Edward Colston must have been an ancestor of the one Thomas Banting's father worked for from 1791 to 1825. Filkins Hall was burnt down in 1876, and was not rebuilt until 1911–12, when Colonel Salle de la Terriere bought it, as I have already described. Before that, and some time after the time of the Colstons, the family of Smith lived there when my grandmother Rachel Swinford, worked for them. In 1896 a tennis club was started and they played at Filkins Hall. It was called The Colston Lawn Tennis Club. I do not know exactly why it was called Colston, as none of the family had been living there for a long time. Somebody asked me if I remembered why, and I told him that the upper classes did not discuss things with us in those days, so they would not have told us. I do know that the tennis players kept their horses in the stables that had been built for Edward Colston in 1810. I have slippers used by his horses in the Museum. I also have a nice picture of Arabella, one of the daughters of Edward Francis Colston, who resided at the Hall when Thomas Banting was a boy. She was buried in Broadwell churchyard, and there is a memorial tablet to her in the church.

I must say a few more words about the stables and coach house. The datestone of 1810 has a dolphin underneath as the dolphin was the Colston crest. I have been told that the Colston family came from Bristol where they had a shipping company, and at the time of the wooden ships the story goes that one of their ships sprung a leak, and a dolphin somehow got fixed in the hole, and saved the ship and the lives of the people who were on it, and they made the Dolphin their crest or coat of arms. Thomas Banting tells us that the silver and the harness, livery buttons, etc. all had the Dolphin on it, and the carriages had it painted on the side.

C. Farmer told me his grandfather helped carry the clock up the stairs of the stables, the maker was Mr Honeybourne of Fairford. The clock has been a boon to the village for many years, and is still going strong. The two stone pillars on the Kencot road were built for the purpose of having a drive down to the bog where they were going to build an artificial lake. This was never done, and there was never a drive made across the park from the house to the pillars. There is a nice old pigeon house near the stables.

Now I will quote some of Thomas Banting's story, which he began in 1846

I, Thomas Banting, was born in the year 1814 on December 20th at six o'clock in the morning at Filkins in the County of Oxford, just five days before the commencement of the Great Frost of sixteen weeks duration, when there was a Fair on the Thames, and the snow reached up to the window of the bedroom in which I was born.

My father was the second son of Thomas Banting, my grandfather who died in 1812. Grandfather was a Blacksmith by trade at Broadwell in Oxfordshire, where the family had resided for many generations. He was the father of sixteen children, but only seven were alive when I was born, my father being the only one that ever married, and I am the only issue of that marriage.

My father was apprenticed to an Ironmonger named Kirby at Wantage in Berkshire in the year 1789, and was obliged to leave on account of the severity of the winter, which had liked to be the cause of his losing the use of his limbs. Not recovering immediately, he was obliged to give up the work and go into gentleman's service. He went to Filkins Hall about 1791 as coachman to E. F. Colston Esq, and lived as such up to about 1825. He rented his house in the village from them as tenant until about 1848.

This history relating to my life may be said to begin early in 1812 — over two years before I was born and a little before the death of my grandfather. A property came to him subject to a mortgage of £150, which required my grandfather to borrow money on an old family house and shop and land at Filkins. My father, thinking to oblige him, contrived with the assistance of my mother, to whom he was not yet married, to advance the sum of £160 on this property.

Then my father had to go to the Isle of Wight with the Colston family for a few months, and on his return he found his father too far gone to settle his affairs about this property. They had already got the money, but my father was always slack in such matters and did not trouble to press the business at that time. He received the rent of the place as interest for twenty-four years, until the premises began falling down for want of repair.

But to return to my mother, she was not thought good enough for my father by his brothers and sisters . . . (who) used every intrigue to annoy her . . . They got me to go and live there and pretended to learn me a trade . . . so I remained until the Colston family Father was living in (interfered). Then I came home and went regularly to school for some years. I done errands for a lady backwards and forwards from Alvescot to the Hall while I was still at school, and at one time and another I managed to save five pounds. I bought a sow in pig with this money and had good luck, she brought eight piglets. My father said he would buy them for eight pounds, but they was seized with fever and all died but one, so I never had a farthing.

. . . About . . . 1828 a gentleman named Vizard took the Hall. He was lawyer to Queen Caroline. With Lord Brougham and Lord Denman they won a trial for her, of which I can just recollect the band coming round and playing at the houses where we lived. Lord Brougham came to the Hall on a visit when he was Lord Chancellor, and gave my father council for nothing in a Will case.

This was a few years before the building of the Union Workhouses. I well remember an incident that happened then. An old man lay ill at a house not far from the Hall called The Old Workhouse. His name was John Hamblin, a Langford man, a maltster by trade. Mr Vizard and his lordship went to visit him. They climbed up a ladder to the room above, and there lay the old man on a bed of straw. This wont do, Vizard, said his lordship, we must alter these things. They were altered a short time afterwards.

Lord Brougham used to go to Cannes in France every winter, and I remember he sent Mr Vizard a cow from there, and so we had the cow and kept it and the family had what milk they liked out of it.

About this time the smallpox broke out in the village, and I and my uncle's apprentice had it together. He had been vaccinated before for the cow pox. I had never had the cow pox, and I had the smallpox very bad. He never had anything, but his arm swelled a little. I grew in height fives inches from the November we had it till the next November. He was never right well afterwards, he had a scorbutic humour come over him. Some said it was owing to the smallpox not coming out. However he lived to get married, but the complaint killed him.

There follow names of the family of Colston and their servants at the time I was a boy, who then resided at the old Hall, and who now mostly lie buried in Broadwell church and churchyard.

Edward Francis Colston Esq. — the father
Mrs Colston, the second wife of the above
Rev. Tom Colston Esq. son of the above
Alexander Colston Esq. son of the above
Charles Colston Esq. son of the above
Miss Arabella Colston, daughter of the above
Miss Sophia Colston, daughter of the above
Miss Fanny Colston, daughter of the above
Miss Luisa Colston, daughter of the above

Mr John Bullock, late huntsman to a Mrs Colston, former owner of the Hall

Mr Thomas Hott, Butler
Thomas Banting, Coachman
John Kirby, Footman
William Burdock, Groom
Mrs Kitty Wheeler, Cook
Elizabeth Musto, Housemaid
Mary Jonsons, Kitchenmaid
David Harris, Gardener
Sarah Crofts, Ladies Maid

Somewhere about this time the last bull was baited in Filkins. There had used to be one always baited on Feast Monday. I can just recollect the last man as was ever whipped in the stocks. His name was Thomas Radway, better known as Old Fielding. He was whipped by the great miller named Purbrick at Filkins Mill, a very strong man who stood over six foot. Once for a wager he undertook that he and his horse would carry round the market place half a load of wheat. He carried two sacks and his horse three sacks, but just as it was accomplished a man patted the horse on the back which caused him to shunt and broke his back. The miller said he would have carried an extra sack himself if he had knowed this was going to happen.

I think it was in November 1830 that the machine breaking and rioting was. Farmers drawed all their four horse power thrashing machines into their grounds away from their homes for fear of having their farms set afire. Every night parties went out somewhere or other to break up the thrashing machines, till at last they all agreed to have a regular riot. All the men of several villages round about met on Southrop bridge by hundreds, and I can just remember hearing the horn being blown before it was scarcely light in the morning. Before night they were all dispersed in all directions. Some got clean away and never came back. Very many went to prison but the ringleaders of that day was never caught. The head man came home many years afterwards and died.

Times were very bad then. I knew 26 able bodied men at work on the roads at one shilling a day. They went to hop skip and jump the greatest part of their time to keep themselves warm in winter.

About 1832 my father took ten acres of arable land and I began to learn to be a farmer, and I was thoroughly devoted to it. The first boy I ever had to drive the plough wore buckskin breeches and he was the last boy I ever knew to wear them, because the old man as made them died soon after. Some years before that time all the labourers and boys never wore anything else. What a difference now — my boy wears a black jacket and a paper collar, although his father has got ten children.

We lived hard, we had barley and wheat ground together for bread, bread being dear. But however I was always of a saving turn. By dealing in pigs and one thing and another I managed to have as much as fifty pounds about 1843 and could have got a good living for myself by then. That troubled the old folks not a little as I was their chief stay, so they thought how they could get my money for fear I should leave them. Father got the Esquire to sell him a house and a piece of land and persuaded me to let him have my money. He said I should have one of the houses, we built two, but I never could get anything any more.

In 1836 a gentleman pretended to purchase Filkins Hall and estate. He was a year or two about it but died before the sale was completed. Then it was again offered for sale, this time in lots by auction at the Bull in Burford, but in consequence of not selling the house first it was all quashed again. In about two years more another gentlemen named Archer purchased it and said he should be here in a fortnight, but again it was abandoned altogether. Then it remained as before for about two years, and then a solicitor named Herbert of Northleach bought it and actually had the deeds and mortgaged them. It cost the family a great deal to get them back again, but he was never heard of afterwards.

1844 was the year of the great blight with the wheat,

and tremendous hailstorms which destroyed the crops round Banbury and other places in Oxfordshire and did a great amount of damage. One man I knew burnt about twenty acres of standing wheat this year. Even the straw was good for nothing. It was either this year or in 1845 when the potato blight commenced. January 1845 will ever be memorable as on the eighth day of January I saw a man mowing a large field of barley in his great-coat on. This was the coldest day I ever knew. There were hundreds of acres of barley got in then, and the government allowed farmers to dry barley at the malthouses before they could use it . . . Coal at this time was two and sixpence a hundred-weight.

In the year 1847 one Feargus O'Connor M.P. bought an estate at Minster Lovell for the Chartists and laid four acres of land to them, and hearing of this estate for sale came over and made a bargain, which was a very great sore to the neighbouring Gentry and he bantering them too hard, when a neighbouring Esquire stept in and bought it much to the mortification of Mr Feargus O'Connor M.P., but I understood he made them pay £500 for disappointing him. Everybody at that time thought it would ruin the place if he bought it, as it was just 30 years ago as he bought the Minster Lovell estate. The little allotments have answered well and are let several of them at £3 per acre, and if he had kept it it would have been a great blessing to this place. Cursed be the man that layeth field to field and house to house (Bible). And now the gentleman as bought the estate began cutting down the timber. The man who bought it this time was Esquire

Harvey who lived at Bradwell Grove. A new tenant
was brought in who put his horses in the big stables.
There was but one way to the Park through our cow
yards and they came in and out at all times. We had
six beautiful cows in calf but one was run over and
another cast her calf, another dwindled, and being hurt
by a lot of cart horses coming in and out loose all the
lot was spoiled.

About the year 1851 there occurred a magnetic
storm in July. We had just returned to work from
dinner in the middle of the day. We had a man and
woman hoeing swedes just over the hedge and I said
to the man that I expected some thunder . . . Then
there came such a vivid flash of lightning like a long
white chain which seemed to fall in a field beyond
where we were. My father had been walking up there
a few minutes before and so I was alarmed about
him, never having seen a flash of lightning without
a cloud before in the daytime. It so happened that
the flash struck down a man at Blackbourton about
a mile beyond us, exactly the direction in which it
appeared to us to fall. His name was Benjamin Clark,
he survived but twenty years later he told me he had
never been right since.

A few years afterwards I noticed some natural
history worth recording. We used to have several
magpies nests every year and as they became old
ones the sparrowhawks took to them and built their
nests in them. Once there was a hedge sparrows nest
under the hawks nest, the young hawks were big
enough to fly in and out, but they and the old hawks

never interfered with the pair of sparrows underneath although the sparrow is their chief food.

I had been renting my farm for 27 years from Mr Price of Burford and worked early and late for nothing at all, what little property I had got went yearly towards paying the rent. In 1876 Mr Price died and next year I gave up the farm after losing nearly £400, although I worked like a horse. By 1878 no end of farmers were in the same case. Now it is 1879 and a wetter season than ever. For four seasons there has been no land cleared and prices of corn are so low that nearly all the farmers are giving up their farms. At the time of writing there is an inquiry by parliament into the existing distress of the farmers, and before long there will be inquiry into the distress of the landlords. There has been a Conservative government with a majority of one hundred and never attempted to do one thing for tenant farmers. They passed an Act to do away with all the turnpikes and put all the expense of the roads on the ratepayers, and one brewer I have heard saves one thousand pounds a year in turnpikes alone.

These are a few extracts from Mr Thomas Banting's history. I remember him well, he lived to be a very old man and died about 1900. He kept pigs and a few hens on a plot of land near the Hadge. I have the smock which he wore in old age and gave to my mother.

CHAPTER
SIX

A Little World

When I was young there was always plenty of people around in Filkins, and a great deal going on. Much of what we needed was made in the village. It was a little world in itself. Nowadays there never seems to be anyone around doing anything.

First of all there were the blacksmiths. They were most important people, and one could write a lot about them as they were capable of doing so many jobs. When we look today in the ironmonger's shop and see the agricultural and gardening tools — in fact nearly all the hardware — we can hardly realize that they were all made by the village blacksmith years ago. In the Museum I have a good collection of forks — garden, hay, straw, stone — all handmade, and carpenters' tools such as chisels, gouges, draw knives, pincers, axes, hammers and even nails made by the blacksmith in those days. He also worked with the wheelwright, making the ironwork for carts and waggons and bonding all the wheels, not only for farm carts but for trucks, barrows and even the first bicycles. He made the shares for the ploughs, and made and fixed and maintained the water pumps, iron or lead. Then all the farm implements he made, hoes, breast ploughs, pick-axes, shovels, shepherds' crooks, billhooks, etc. He made all the masons' tools, which I shall describe later. Then there was the ironmongery he made for the builder. Besides nails of different lengths he made nuts and bolts, hinges of all kinds large or small, door latches, bolts and handles, iron window frames with lead lights, pokers, tongs and shovels for the fireplace. Anything in iron was made by the blacksmith, even the sheep bells and cow bells. He would be the pig ringer and sometimes the pig butcher. He would also ring the bulls for the farmers. He was interested in all the village affairs, and he was willing to help in every way.

When I was a boy we had two blacksmiths' shops, Mr Holloway and Mr Trinder, who both employed one or two other smiths and a striker. The striker was the man who used the heavy sledge hammer to beat the lumps of iron flat. A good striker helped the blacksmith a lot, as in those days they could not buy rods and bars of the right size as they can today. They had to beat it from a lump of iron called a rose, which varied in size, so they hotted it and cut off a piece the size they needed for the job they were doing. They also made most of the tools they themselves used.

The house next to the Museum used to be a blacksmith's and wheelwright's shop. A man named Cockbill first ran the business. In the old parish book it says "Paid Mr Cockbill for coffin 10/– shroud 1/6 and 3/6 for beer for the funeral." I remember the old sawpit being filled in where they cut out the coffin boards from elm trees. I did some work there a few years ago, and under the floorboards I found some old coffin furniture.

There was black tin, a bit rusty, and real tin pressed out into silver angels.

Then Mr Holloway took over the premises and continued the business. He was a clever man. He made the altar rail in the church, the grapes were made from horseshoe nails. When bicycles came in he started a cycle shop, repairing and letting out bicycles at sixpence an hour. This was the post office at one time, as I have said, and when Mr Holloway died his daughter carried it on. I have a picture of Mr Holloway, sitting in a Bath chair. He did not make the carriage itself, he altered it so that you could sit and turn the handle to make the wheels go round. It was for Jesse Farmer's father. Mr Holloway was a policeman before he became a blacksmith, he was also the sexton and rang the church bells.

The other blacksmith, Mr Trinder, had a brother who was a carpenter and wheelwright. You could ask them to make just what you wanted. You had to ask before you wanted it, of course, as they would not work extra time after their ordinary long day, but you did not have to wait long as Trinder and Holloway worked in together and handed jobs on. The first smithy was in the house opposite my present cottage, at the end of what was then the village green before the church was built. Mr F. Trinder was the smith. Then it moved to the house next door to The Bull Inn. The horses went through The Bull Inn yard to be shod, of course they always arranged not to have too many at a time. John Garne had twelve horses, Glover at Moat Farm two or three, Pryor at Pear Tree about four, and Peacock Farm had several. Many people had a trap with a horse, pony or donkey, and these all had to be shod. I remember how someone would mow the side of the road for food for his animal and be summonsed, as the owner of the adjoining field paid rates for the roadside, as I have said. The fine would be sixpence.

We have only one blacksmith's shop in our village today, the son of Mr F. Trinder, who also has his son Dennis working with him. They still make a few farm implements such as harrows, and repair farm machinery, and they also make iron gates, and do pipe work for hot and cold baths.

The village carpenter and wheelwright generally worked together in the one business, together with undertaking and some building. Mr W. Trinder ran a business on these lines in our village for some years. His yard and shops were opposite The Five Alls Inn, in the place which was formerly The Fox Inn. They had a pit where they used to cut up trees by hand. Sawing up into boards was hard work, and these men worked together in pairs, travelling from place to place where there was sawing to be done, taking their saws with them. The men who were employed were all handy men and would help do anything. They repaired the carts and waggons and all wooden wheels, and also farm buildings and cottages, doing roofs, walls, painting and decorating, and of course any woodwork such as mending wheelbarrows, doors, odd pieces of furniture, etc. A small general business like this meant having a lot of tools, and of course they had to keep some of the old tools for matching up with the old work when repairing. This business was run without any machinery, everything being done by hand. Mr W. Trinder died in 1928, and I am afraid the old wheelwright is gone for ever.

There was plenty of work with all the sheep on the Downs for our two hurdle makers, Frederick and Henry Jones, who were brothers. Frederick worked regularly for Mr John Garne, making hurdles and gates, repairing fences and carts and waggons. His workshop was in Mr Garne's orchard. All fencing was done with wooden posts and rails, as this was before fencing wire was used. Henry Jones worked part time at Langford Downs Farm and part time at Little Faringdon Farm. The willow trees in the field near the stream were planted on purpose for making hurdles and gates and fencing. A certain number were cut every year, so that it worked out that each tree had seven years growth before it was cut again. The willow poles when rendered down made very good hurdles as they were light and strong. I do not think there has been a hurdle made in the village for a good many years now. Few hurdles are used on the farms today, wire netting and electric fencing having taken their place.

Painting was a different trade in the last century to what it is today, as the painter had to grind his own paint. I have two grinding stones in the Museum used by men in Filkins in my youth. The painter would have a flat stone like a table on which he put his oil, turps, linseed and then his different coloured powder. This he rubbed with another hard stone called a painter's grinding stone. When the powder was well rubbed into the oil, the white or red lead was added and well rubbed again. Then it was strained, and what was left in the strainer was rubbed again and again until it all went through the strainer. Of course this all took a great deal of time. Our painters also made their own putty by smashing up whiting and mixing linseed oil with the powder. This was stored in oak tubs ready for use. Later came a paint grinder something like a sausage machine, where they filled the hopper and turned the handle, and the paint ran out of the spout. These were very handy, as all the old paint skins could be ground up again. Painters also boiled linseed oil, which they kept in barrels and used for different jobs. Another of the painter's jobs was to make the lead bars in the leaded light windows. This was done by first melting lead and running it into narrow strips. Then with a machine of two wheels, with a groove in each wheel the shape of the lead bar that was wanted, a handle was turned and the bar came out between the two wheels. This was drawn along the bench and cut off in lengths, and stored by for use. Now all this labour is done away with, as paint is bought ready made, also putty and windows.

The tin and copper smiths worked as one trade in our village, and were generally known as tinkers. The work they did was to make tin and copper pots, kettles, jugs, cans, Dutch ovens, baking tins, etc. Dutch ovens were used in the home for roasting small birds or rashers of bacon, with a piece of bread underneath to catch the fat. The tinkers also made the spouting, rainwater heads and downpipes. I have some of these rainwater pipes in the Museum, and some very good work was put into them. The different shapes are all very interesting, and some had decorations such as the star or the thistle. Every year they went to the big houses and re-tinned the copper utensils used for cooking, putting a new lining of tin inside. We had a travelling tinker from Bampton who came round the villages pushing a truck loaded with these utensils for sale, also saucepan lids and pot lids, and if he had not got a lid the right size he would bring one for you the next time he came. I think the last tin smith, named Richards, came from Bampton.

We had two shoemakers in the village when I was a boy. One was Mr C. Booker. He first lived in one of a beautiful row of old cottages with fine gables and roofs. However, in 1899, the time I left school, as the land belonged to Mr W. H. Fox Esq. of Bradwell Grove, he built a reading room there and let it to the village for one shilling per year. So Charles Booker moved to Broughton, where his cottage is still called Bookers Cottage. He made the first pair of shoes I ever had, so my mother told me. I remember him well. The boots he made were quite straight and you could wear them on either foot, they were heavy but they wore well.

The shoemakers did not like to be called cobblers. I remember my father who suffered with chapped hands used to get some cobbler's wax and hot it in a candle and drop it in the cracks. He said it stopped them getting bigger. Once he sent me down to Booker's and I knocked at the door and said "A pennyworth of cobbler's wax, please." He said "Who sent you for this?" and I said "My father". He said "Go back and tell him we have only got shoemaker's wax." You can guess this caused a bit of fun, but I always thought of the right word after that. Mr Booker had two brothers working for him. I suppose the boots and shoes they made were rather ugly, but they put some good materials into them, and Mr Booker often bragged that he could stitch sixteen to the inch, which I think was very good for hand stitching. When he had finished a pair of heavy working boots he would bring them along and say "I have brought your boy's boots and I have put plenty of steel on them. They will be 10/– to you, but for anybody else they would be 10/6d. Don't say anything to anybody, and here's a good strong pair of laces to put in them." He told the same story to everybody.

Mr Booker had a shoes' club where a family could pay sixpence a week, and when they had enough on the card they could have a pair of shoes for anybody in the family. We had to be measured every time. I still have his rule in the Museum, and his tools and cobbler's bench. He used to deliver the letters in the village and sell a few vegetables as a sideline. He said it all helped to keep the wolf from the door and clear the bad debts that he owed. He was a quiet man and everybody liked him. I remember him setting off with a handkerchief bundle over his shoulder full of old and new boots, some he had made and some he had repaired, and delivering them and bringing back more to be repaired, or an order for some new ones. His journey on Saturday night was to Kencot, Broadwell and Langford. If the taking was very good he would call at The Crown Inn at Langford, have one drink and then home.

The other shoemaker was Mr G. Hazell, who lived in Hazells Lane where we lived, and which was named after him. I remember the house was built specially for a shoemaker's shop at the end of the lane, with the cream coloured Bradwell Grove stones. It is still there. I remember leaning on the wall and looking at the three men at work. Old Mr Hazell would come out and say "What do you want?" and we would say "A bit of leather for my sling", and he would go and fetch us a piece, and say "Now mind, don't get breaking the windows." He used to make a better shaped boot than Mr Booker, and lighter too, suitable for Sundays, if one could afford to buy them, as they were a bit dearer. He also made heavy ones of kip leather, and after you had been in the wet grass a few times they got very hard, and it was a job to get them on in the morning. As I have already said, the old men had a remedy for this. They would get the pigs' tails and hot them by the fire and rub the fat on the boots to soften them. As the tails wore down bits were cut off the end until they were used up. Mr Hazell, too, used to go off with his bundle over his shoulder to deliver his goods in the evening, and later I remember he had a tricycle with a carrier on the back. My father told me he could remember when there were four shoemakers in Filkins. The old notice board is still over the front door, and one can still just read "G. Hazell. Shoemaker". I hope it will not be taken down. Mr Hazell died about 1903, and Mr Booker died about 1934. This was the end of the boot and shoemakers in the village. Of course we have the menders still, but rubber boots and rubber soles are gradually putting them out of business.

There used to be a tailor's shop in Filkins in the cottage at the end of Cross Tree Lane. I do not remember this myself, but I do remember a tailor at Broughton named Preston, they called him Bodkin. He was a very good tailor when he would work, but he was very fond of the drink and would not work if he had any money, so his business went and he went too, to live at Brize Norton as ostler at a public house. Then a man called Compton from Broadwell used to do work for Filkins people. I have been over with parcels and fetched some back a good many times. I have three pairs of tailor's scissors in the Museum. These belonged to a Filkins tailor and I have heard his name but have forgotten it. There was also a tailor who travelled from the Manchester-Liverpool Ship Canal, and made corduroy trousers which were called Canal Trousers. They had three thick lines and one narrow. He measured you with a two-foot rule and they were always a perfect fit. He also made suits, but the working men could not manage to get a whole new suit. They got a pair of breeches, and then their wives made them smocks which they wore over their shirts. Of course nearly everybody carried an umbrella in those days. The old saying was that you could tell a Filkins man because he always carried an umbrella.

The smocks were usually made of heavy Irish linen, and were very warm and kept out the rain. They were made in different designs, some to pull over the head like a modern pullover, and some to button down the front. The smocking was the same back and front, so that when the smock was dirty you could wear it the other way round. There were Shepherds' smocks and Carters' smocks and Woodmans' smocks and Masons' smocks. The Woodmans' smock had trees done in herringbone, and the Masons' had very little smocking as the stone dust lodged in it. I can remember several old men

109

wearing them when I was a boy. Then corduroy began to be used more, and ready-made clothes came into the shops, and nearly all the workers wore cord trousers, waistcoats and jackets, and smocks were not worn much and gradually disappeared. Instead, for summer wear a light jacket made of linen with a large hare pocket in it was brought out. This was called a slop, and I have one of them in the Museum. As wages rose workers were able to dress better, and a mason wore cord trousers, a moleskin waistcoat and a Chipping Norton tweed jacket. Some managed to buy a tweed suit for Sundays.

When I was a boy, the upper and middle class men wore top hats for their best. I can remember them going to church with them on. Then came the bowler which was worn by most men. I have one now that I wore when I was a young man. The first caps were made by the local tailors. My father told me that when he was a boy the working men wore a hat that was made of a dark felt mixed with straw, the shape like a bell, and they called them cow dung hats. Straw hats something like Eton schoolboys' hats were worn in summer.

Of course there was plenty going on in Filkins besides work. For one thing, there was fighting. Every village had what was called a best man at fighting, and sometimes the best man in one village was expected to take on the best man in another village. These met sometimes by accident and sometimes by arrangement, but they met somehow, and this was generally the beginning of a lot more fighting brought on by arguments about the fight. I have heard my father and other men talk about a man at Broughton named Palmer who was a wonderful fighter.

He was very tall with long arms. It was said that he could stand upright and buckle his gaiter at the knee without bending down, so he must have had a very long reach. At this time a gentleman lived at Broughton Hall named Goshen. He had his business in London and did not get down very often, but when he came he brought some of his friends, and a fighter too, to have a go at Palmer. This used to take place on the front lawn on Sunday afternoon to amuse these gentlemen. Of course Palmer got the worst of it sometimes, but he generally gave as good as he got, and he was paid very well for the entertainment given.

When the Bibury races were on there was always a lot of fighting there, and Palmer was generally amongst it. I heard from a farmer, who worked at Oxleaze Farm and had the half day off to go to the races, that as soon as Palmer got there someone came up to him and said "They have brought one especially for you today, Palmer." "All right, I'll have a bit of dinner first, then you can bring him along," said Palmer. So they stripped among the caravans and started to fight. After a few minutes sparring Palmer let go, and hit the other fellow a blow on the forehead and the skin fell down over his eyes. This finished the fight, and as Palmer was on his own without friends they tried to mob him. He stood with his back to a caravan wheel and knocked them down as fast as they could come. This was the last fight Palmer had at Bibury. He went to the races as usual, but nobody interfered with him after that.

Another man I would like to mention was Tommy Robbins. He was a little hunchback, only about four feet six inches tall. I remember him. If you stood behind him you could only see the top of his head, but he was very strong. His trick was to throw men over his back, and I have heard big men say that they would not have a second go at him if they could help. I heard a story about a cheapjack from Northleach (a cheapjack was a hawker who laid out his goods on the grass and auctioned them). He had a go at Tommy and was thrown twice and that was enough, but he promised he would meet Tommy again one day. Then one night when he walked into The Lamb someone asked him if he was looking for Tommy Robbins. He said "No, but I am not afraid of him." So they went to Tommy's house and told him the cheapjack was in The Lamb. Tommy had gone to bed, but he looked out of the window and said "All right, I'll be down in a few minutes." When he walked into The Lamb and shouted, the cheapjack stood up and said "I don't want to fight you, Tommy, I want to get home before morning, so let's have some beer and say no more about it." So he paid for plenty of beer.

When boys met boys from other villages there was often a fight. I remember I was often sent to Broadwell to a tailor to fetch some clothes or take some to be repaired. When we met the Broadwell boys we would shout —

Broadwell scrubs, Broadwell scrubs,
Born in buckets and christened in tubs.

Sometimes we ran away, and sometimes we stood our ground if there were not too many of them, and finished with a fight, and when we parted we threw stones at one another and called out bad names. There is not much fighting these days or quarrelling between the villages as there was years ago.

Football started in Filkins about 1898, when Alf Spiers came to live at The Lamb Inn. He was an old footballer from Lechlade, and he brought with him the first football. I remember a few of the young men used to go out in the Gassons and kick it about, and of course we boys joined in when we could. When we saw them head the ball we thought it was wonderful, and tried to copy them. Mr Spiers kept a lot of pigs, and he told us that if we would fill up the tubs and tanks with water we could have the football for two hours. This was a lot of work as we had to pump up the water and carry it out into the field in all the buckets and water cans we could find. It took us all morning, and then we had the ball for the afternoon.

We were getting older now and we wanted a ball of our own, so we got together and decided we would save our pennies and get one before the winter. We went and talked with someone who could bring a football back from Witney. He said he would find out how much it would be and let us know. We went and saw him again, and he told us he could let us have one for 5s., so we gave the order for him to bring it back. On the following Thursday we were all there waiting for him, and he told us it would be 5s.6d., and he would not let us have it without the money. Some of us said we would go home and ask for another penny. Some of us got a penny and some had a good hiding instead. We managed to get another fourpence, and found him and promised him the other twopence the next week, but no, he would not let us have it, and told us not to come and bother him again unless we had 5s.6d.

So off we went down the village. By the shop by the bridge lived a man called Timbrell. He came out to talk to us and we told him what the carrier had said. He said "Give me your 5s.4d. and I will get you one by return of post", and this we did. Next we went back to the carrier and he came out and said "Then you have got the money for the ball." We said no, we had come to tell him that someone else was getting us a football, and he could take his back. He tried to persuade us to have it, but we told him it was too late. I remember how we had to go down about 5.30 pm to fetch the ball when it arrived, and how we all ran up the street with it, shouting, into the Gassons. It was a nice moonlight night, and we were kicking the first football about that was our own. We spent every bit of time we had at football. Ken Woodman put his knee out, Jack Rouse hurt his arm, someone got fighting about it and this meant black eyes, our mothers said it wore our boots out, and some told their boys not to play as it was such a dangerous game, but for all that we still carried on, and soon our mothers and fathers came and watched us, and a team began to form.

In 1903 we played our first match, it was on Good Friday. We played Lechlade Second XI in Taylors Close, where the village centre now stands. We had no goal-posts or outside, and when the ball was kicked into the wall it was a throw-in. We did not know the rules of the game, but I think everyone who played and those who watched enjoyed it very much. We played football all the summer if we could find a pitch to play on. That was difficult at times, and we were expecting the police. I remember one moonlight night we were playing on the Moors, and the policeman was waiting in the hedge for the ball to go that way. He sprung out and got it and kept it for a week. He tried to get the farmer to summons us, but he would not, so he gave us the ball back. The next year we began better equipped. Some of us bought football jerseys and some boots.

I remember walking to Lechlade with three or four others to see a match, and also with the intention of buying some boots, as we had heard that Edmonds had some in. We had Tom Flux with us. He was deaf and dumb and a very good player, as he had learnt football at school in Birmingham. Four of us bought boots, including Tom Flux, who had six toes on one foot and five on the other. When we got home we went into the reading room to show our boots, and somebody noticed that Tom Flux's boots had different toecaps. We laughed at him, but he turned his boots upside down and pointed his finger, and we saw that he had got one size seven, and one size eight for the foot with six toes, so he had the laugh on us all right. We could talk to him very well by signs, and he could do lip reading, but as he could not hear the referee's whistle he often kept going for some time, until someone could get in front of him and beckon to him to stop.

There were not many football teams about then, and we had not got the money to hire a horse and trap to go further afield. We used to walk to Lechlade to play, have a sixpenny tea at Evans and a look round Lechlade, and then walk home. We generally started back together, but by the time we got home we were a long way apart, all tired out. We kept improving every year, and I remember the first game we were not beaten in, it was a draw, 1–1, against Brize Norton. I was working at The Swan Inn, Bibury at the time. I left work at 11 am, walked ten miles back to Filkins and started football at 2.30 pm. It was a very wet day, and I remember having the cramp badly in the night. Brize Norton was also the first team we beat, 2–0. I remember when we got back and told the news, it was wonderful.

In these days a lot of our players worked on farms until five o'clock on Saturday, which meant they had to lose half a day's work. The farmers did not like the men to go either, as it sometimes meant the horses had to be in the stable, or if the man was with the sheep or cattle it meant putting another man in his place. I remember Jack Rouse was working for a farmer at Little Faringdon, and one Saturday morning the farmer went into the field to pay him where he was at plough. Jack said "Master, I want the half day off this afternoon." "What, to go to the football! I should think thee bist daft. No, you stop and get on with this ploughing, and mind you don't bring those horses in at dinner time." "All right," said Jack, and when dinner time came he stopped the plough, unharnessed the horses, put the harness under the hedge and turned the horses out in the field, and went off to football. He never went back again to work for that farmer. This story got around and worried the farmers, and they soon realized it was no good trying to stop football this way. So the men were let off, but they had to lose the half day's pay.

Our team still improved, and we were recognized as one of the best around and won most of our matches, and spectators came from other villages to see us play. I have seen over two hundred people watching us in the Moors. In 1906 I had an invitation to go and play for Lechlade, which was a great honour. I did not want to go but my pals persuaded me. I played for them until 1911 when I got married. Filkins still ran a very good team until the 1914 War started. After the War we ran a good team for a few years. Then my brother Joe, and Billy Merchant, two of our best players, went to play for Witney Town. This seemed to take effect, and there was less interest and the team gradually dwindled to nothing. Today boys seem to me more content to watch others play than play themselves. Although they have better opportunities now than we had in our day, I don't think football in Filkins is as good as it was in 1904 to 1920.

Like most villages Filkins had a good cricket team. From 1890 I remember they played full day matches from 11 am to 6.30 pm. We schoolboys used to run up from school at dinner time to see the last hour before they went to lunch at 1 pm, and we were often late back for school. The old cricket pitch was in the park near the Clock Ground, and there was a wooden pavilion which stood under the row of large elm trees. Cricket was the only team game then, as football had not yet come to the village. Our schoolmaster had a son who was a schoolmaster in London, and every summer he used to bring about eighteen friends down to Filkins for their holiday, and they were all good cricketers. They lodged in Filkins and played all the villages around. Nearly every day they had a match on, and they were noted for their good sportsmanship. After the match they were capable of giving a good concert. They were called the London Ramblers, and we looked forward to their visit every year.

As far as cricket was concerned, we boys had a rough time. We made our own bats from the butt end of a withy pole, and the stumps and bails were whittled out with our pocket knives, but the worst job was to find somewhere to play. Often the policeman was on our track, and as soon as we started to play he was there. If he got hold of any of our equipment we never got it back, so we arranged that each one should pick up what he could before running away. I think I should mention Jessop, the Gloucestershire hard hitter. He was a schoolmaster at Burford Grammar School, and often played in the villages around here. It was a wonderful feat for the one who could get him out. The ball used was gutta-percha, something like very hard rubber, and heavy. In about 1908 we had a very good team, but still a job to get a field. Then a man named Holland bought Broughton Hall, and he was interested in cricket. He made us a pitch in the Dry Ground in front of the Hall, and bought us new bats and some other equipment including nets, which we used to keep in the saddle room at the stables, which was handy. But unfortunately Mr Holland died suddenly, and the house was sold to Mr Hardcastle. The next spring we called a meeting, and appointed officials to go and fetch our equipment and clean out the saddle room, but Mr Hardcastle told them it now belonged to him, and would not let them take it. This finished the cricket club. People tried to start it again several times, but it was never successful. Mr Hardcastle was a real old-fashioned customer. When he was ninety-one he ordered a new car. One day he came up his drive with his thumb stick to Broughton bridge over the mill stream where we boys were leaning over the wall, and he said "Looking at my fish, are you?" I said "Is that your water?" and he said "Swinford, you're a dangerous person."

Another popular game was quoits. Each public house had its quoit bed, made by digging a hole about a yard square and filling it with clay, the beds about twenty yards apart. In the centre of the bed was stuck a peg or pin, and the game was to throw your quoit over the pin or as near to it as you could. If you threw your quoit over the pin it was called a ringer and counted two, and if you had one nearer than the others you scored one more. The game could be played with one or two on each side. When you played one a side, you changed ends after each throw, and your second throw was from the other end, but when you played two a side you stayed at the same end all the time, throwing them back to one another. This game was played for beer. I have heard my father say that he would go to The Lamb with only a penny, buy half a pint, challenge the landlord to quoits and win enough beer to last him all day. The beds had to be watered in summer to keep them moist, so that the quoits would stick in. We boys used to get a penny for carrying water and putting wet sacks over the beds. I have several sets of quoits in the Museum which were used in our pubs.

Another local event was the Flower Show, which the village agreed on after the 1914–18 War. A meeting was held in 1920 and it was settled to hold the show in about the middle of July. We had a good show for several years. Sir Stafford Cripps gave a silver cup for the person who won the most number of points, and as I have mentioned, my father won it for three successive years and so won it outright. My brother Fred has it now. Just before the last war started, people lost their interest in it and it fell through. The British Legion started it going again, but there does not seem the interest taken now that there used to be.

In the past every village had its team of Morris dancers, and although I don't remember a Filkins team in my time, I have heard that earlier they had a very good team here, of which my father's uncle, Job Farmer, was captain for many years. I have a piece of ribbon in the Museum he wore round his knee. He danced at the party at Broughton Hall for Queen Victoria's Coronation. I also have the knife with the stagshorn handle he used on that occasion to help carve the Coronation joints. I have heard that in the old days every boy of six years understood Morris dances. They used to practise all the year round, and then about nine days before Whitsun they would travel for about thirty miles around. In Whitsun week they would start on Monday and not come home until the following Sunday, sleeping in stables or lofts, and not taking their clothes or boots off. They had plenty of beer, and were not fit for much work the following week with their sore feet and bad stomachs, so that meant another week off.

Every year during the week before Christmas and the week after, Squire Fox used to have people come for shooting, and we would go beating for them. At one o'clock we all went along to the lodge at Bradwell Grove (the cottage which is still there on the roadside) to have dinner. It was all laid up inside for the gentry, while we had our dinner outside. There were big milk churns full of bird soup — they put everything into it, pheasants, partridges, rabbits and hares. You had a pint of beer with your soup, but if you were teetotal you got an extra ladle of soup. They had eleven keepers on the job, and even had the police out to see there was no poaching. But I generally managed to hide a pheasant in my inside pocket, and when they lined up the birds that had been shot, with the beaters standing behind them, I always stood next to a policeman and talked to him all the time, so he was less likely to search me. In that way I never got caught.

CHAPTER SEVEN

Feasts, Festivals, People

Besides sports and games, our great entertainment was the Feasts. Filkins Feast was held on the first Sunday after the 11th October, followed by a general holiday on the Monday. This was when you got a good look at all the newcomers to the village, the people who had been taken on at the Michaelmas Hiring Fair to work on the farms. There were swings and roundabouts and stalls and a cheapjack who would auction things. My mother got a laundry basket with a whole dinner service for six shillings. It was the gypsies, mostly, who kept it going. They were at the end of Hazells Lane, where the cemetery is now. I used to catch them hedgehogs, as I knew where they wintered in the stone walls, under the ledges. I got a penny a hedgehog. The Fair was held in the Gassons, which was all open ground then, and where the bus shelter now is they had coconut shies.

I have heard that years ago they roasted an ox on Filkins Feast day, and also baited a bull. Thomas Banting's history, already mentioned, says that the last bull was baited in Filkins in 1828. The Monday was also a great day for Morris dancing.

Most of the Feast Days were held by the Red, White and Blue Club, and all in Whit week — Alvescot on Monday, Filkins on Tuesday, Langford on Wednesday, Clanfield on Thursday and Leafield on Friday and Saturday. The society known as the Red, White and Blue Club was established on 19th May 1879. My father's name was among the first seventeen members. By the following May they had £14.11s.8d. in funds, and by 1907 there were eighty-four members, and it was made into a Life Club. The purpose of the Club was to help poor people. If you were ill and could not work you could collect up to 10s.6d. a week. If you died they paid £4 to your next of kin towards funeral expenses, and if your wife died you received £2 towards a respectable internment. If you got ill and were not expected to get better you got so much a week for life, like a pension. Every four weeks you paid 2s. into the club, and an extra 3d to pay for the meeting house at The Lamb or Bull Inn. You got an eight-sided token made of zinc and engraved by the members themselves, and when there was a meeting you gave it to the landlord of the inn, and you got three pennyworth of beer or baccy.

You got your Club money sent to you wherever you were, however far away from the village. Your parents might go on paying for you, these were called "kept benefits". You got a letter from the hospital or the doctor saying you were unfit for work, and sent it to the Club Secretary, and you got free medical attendance and medicine. The Club was only for men, as men and women did not mix as they do now. I have the Filkins Club flag in the Museum. The Langford flag had True Britons on it. The Clubs stopped in 1912 when Lloyd George's scheme came along.

I have been reading one of the old rule books, and I will write down a few of the rules which I think are interesting

That a box be provided for the funds of the Society with three different locks and keys affixed thereto, each Steward to keep one key and the Secretary one. That no member be allowed any relief from the Society whose illness is brought on by fighting, wrestling or at his own instigation. That if any club member enter the club room intoxicated, or shall be heard to curse, swear, or to strike, collar or utter abusive, threatening, seditious, treasonable or blasphemous language he shall forfeit one shilling. That the Landlord do keep a good fire in the club room in the winter season or forfeit 2/6d.

On Whit Tuesday, as I said, Filkins Club Feast was held, and every member was expected to attend on or before ten o'clock and walk in procession to and from the parish church without smoking, and attend Divine Service, or forfeit sixpence. If absent the whole day he had to forfeit one shilling, but any member who could not attend could send a relative or friend (a respectable person) in his place, who was subject to the same rules. Old George Cook was generally sheep-shearing at this time, and he would ask me to go in his place.

The day started with the arrival of the band. The

Club Secretary had advertised for a band, asking for an estimate, which was generally £2.10s. or £3. At about nine o'clock they were met by the stewards and flag men at the entrance of the village, and marched playing to the club room. The barrels of beer had already been tapped, the bread and cheese were ready, and this was handed round to the band and the Club members, each member wearing a red, white and blue rosette in his jacket. As they fell in behind the band to march to church, each member passed the Secretary and put sixpence in the box for him, and another twopence for the women who were cooking the meal. At the service we had the same sermon every year.

Then came the main event, the dinner, which was held in a large tent in the Gassons. Each member brought his own knife, fork and spoon. The great joints of mutton and beef were brought up from the bakehouse in a handbarrow borrowed from the wheelwright by an old fellow called Jimmy. He got very cross if anyone else tried to get hold of this job, as they gave him a free dinner for it. Cabbage was the main thing with the meat, besides potatoes. We always pulled our cabbages fresh, early on Whit Tuesday, and if there were not enough in Filkins we fetched some from another village. The women cooked the cabbages and potatoes in huge coppers. I remember particularly the puddings, as they were full of fruit. There was also plenty of beer and lemonade. A special table was laid for the invited guests — the parson, Mr John Garne from the farm house, Mr C. Cook from the mill, and sometimes our MP. The President then asked the parson to say grace. As there were three clubs at Leafield, there

125

were three dinners going on at once, and the parson could only go to one, and there was nobody to say grace at the other two. I remember one year when they asked if anyone would say it, nobody made a move. Then one old chap got up, but he could not think of any grace, so he said "Same as 'twas last year, Amen", and sat down again.

After a good meal the Secretary would report on the Club finances, etc., then he was thanked and everyone clapped, then special invited guests would say a few words, and the band would strike up "For He's a Jolly Good Fellow" after each one had spoken. Then a toast to the Club, and the Queen (or King), then the National Anthem, and that finished another Club dinner. But the Feast was not nearly over. The band played around the village, with the flag man in front, and the two stewards with their money boxes making a collection, and carrying staffs with a bunch of flowers tied on top, one of which was generally the old double red peony. Next the band came back to the club room where they had more beer, and bread and cheese or meat. At about 7 pm seats were brought out onto the grass for the band, and they played dance music until 9 pm, then the National Anthem, and then they packed up. All this time the Fair was going strong, with stalls and swing boats and sometimes roundabouts. If the landlord at The Lamb was new and did not want to bother, the Club was held at The Bull. Sometimes the Club was not satisfied with the conditions, so they changed to the other pub. Club day was when members who had left the village and gone away to work came home to see their parents.

It was a day to look forward to, as for many it was the only time in the year when they saw their friends

Now I will try and recall some memories of some of the characters of men and women who lived in our village. For instance there was Jimmy Clack who had a wooden leg. While pulling down some old buildings at Goodfellows a stone wall fell on him, crushing his leg. They sent for the doctor and carried him home on a hurdle, and he sang songs going up the village. When the doctor arrived on horseback he said there was only one thing to do and that was to take off the leg, as it was so badly smashed, so they arranged to do it in his house. The doctor told his wife to get a strong table and two men, while he went back to Burford and fetched some tools. They tied Jimmy to the table and two men held him, while the doctor amputated the leg. This was done without putting Jimmy to sleep, and the doctor said he never knew a man with such a strong constitution. John Farmer who helped to do the operation told me this story. I remember Jimmy very well. He worked on the roads, and we boys had a lot of fun with him, and he always enjoyed it. He could not run after us, but if he did catch us unawares he could hold us tight, but he never hurt us. He was noted for his strength. He never liked the police, and if he was in The Lamb Inn and the policeman looked in, Jimmy would start singing —

> Champion Jimmy is my name,
> Knocking down bobbies is my game!

This annoyed the policeman and he told Jimmy he would put him outside, but when he went towards him Jimmy shot out his wooden leg, and he could not get near him. Jimmy was summonsed several times for this game of his, and had to pay, as he was insulting a policeman while doing his duty.

At the Club dinner our Member of Parliament was invited, and when he shook hands with the members, Jimmy said "I knowed 'twas you or somebody else as soon as I seed thee, sir." Jimmy had two wooden legs, one for Sundays and one for work. One day while working in the quarry up the College road the pickaxe glanced off a rock and hit his wooden leg and broke it. So he said to Harry Puffitt who was working with him "Harry, go down home and ask my wife to let you have my Sunday leg." Jimmy had a donkey and cart to take him to work when he was working outside the village. When his wife died he went to live with his son at Kencot. He was a lot of trouble, and at last he was sent to the workhouse at Faringdon, where he died at the age of ninety-one. He could neither read or write, but he could reckon up well. You could ask him how many barley corns there were in five yards. He reckoned three to an inch, and he generally got the right answer.

Then there was the Cook family, three brothers, Mark, Sam and George, and one sister named Ellen. Ellen was never married. She spent most of her time in service, and had a little cottage of her own where she came to live in her old age. The three brothers had a habit of talking to themselves quite loudly. When somebody asked George why he talked to himself he said, "'Tis the only sensible man I can talk to." He had a pony and trap which he used to let out, and several allotments where he kept pigs, and which he cultivated with the help of his pony whose name was Tom. Somebody said to George one day "Old Tom is a good pony." George said "Yes, he can do anything, plough, harrow, drill, drag and trapwork. There is some Russian blood in him." George never made much out of his land and pigs, and always seemed in debt. He was a good sheep shearer and in great demand at shearing time, when he earned himself a good bit of money and got straight, but he was soon in trouble again, although he seemed always at work. He went very funny toward the end and was taken to the asylum, where he died.

Mark had a mule, and he tried to farm a bit of land, but he was no better than George. Then he went in for poultry, and when he picked up the first few eggs he ran indoors and shouted to his daughter "Luce, put the rasher waggon on the fire and we'll have some fried eggs and bacon." Poultry keeping did not last very long, as he ate all the profits. Smallholdings were not encouraged by the upper class. A lot of men tried it, but could not get on.

Sam worked as a general labourer, stone digging, navvying or doing farm work. He and George were with the last party to go up to London haymaking. Sam had a housekeeper named Martha. One day she made some broth and put some off the top in a basin for Sam, and had the bottom herself. Sam noticed this, and said to her "Martha, I likes the tops of the beer, but I likes the bottom of the broth." Their father's name was Mark too. I do not remember him but I have heard a lot about him, as he was noted for making up poems. He could not write them himself, and I am afraid a lot of them

129

have been lost, but I had two given to me lately, one about the fire at Filkins Hall, and one about the shop at Broughton Bridge, part of which is in Chapter Four.

Billy Puffitt was a Filkins man, but he had no home. He slept in barns or under ricks, and I heard him say he had not seen a bed for thirty years. He carried his food about with him in an old flag basket. He used to walk into the pub soon after 6 am and have a pint of beer and some bread and cheese or bacon. Then he was ready to walk to Langford Downs, where he worked regularly, taking with him another pint of beer for his lunch and dinner. On his way back he called in at the shop and bought some lard and bacon or cheese, then to the bakehouse for a loaf, then to The Lamb Inn where he had some beer until 10 pm. When the pub closed he went to his sleeping place. People had pity on him, and would cook his bacon and often give him a few vegetables and make him a cup of tea, but he was never a beggar, and was civil with everybody. He kept himself clean although he was sleeping so rough, and would pay someone to wash his shirt. He did not smoke, and the farmers were not too hard on him if they caught him sleeping in their buildings.

As time went on Billy got very bent, and his feet were bad and he had a job to get about, but he kept on going to work as long as he could. Mrs Kerry who lived at The Lamb Inn told me that one Christmas Billy was there, and as they had a piece of Christmas pudding left she thought she would warm it up and take it into him. He thanked her for it, but as she was coming out of the door she heard him say "Look out guts, here's a stranger coming." He gradually got worse and was taken to the workhouse where he died at about seventy years old. Billy seemed quite happy living this strange life. He never quarrelled with anybody. When the pubs were closed on Sundays he would walk about the roads until they opened, having a chat with anyone he met. There have been Puffitts for a long time in Filkins. For instance, in the Parish Book for 1798, it says — Feb 13th: Mary Puffett, her husband walked off 1/–.

Bill Larner of Sherborne was a mason who worked with me. He talked a lot, but did not think of what he was saying, and often got his conversation muddled up. One morning he said to me "George, we be going to have another baker. I went to cut a loaf this morning and there was a great hole in it. I'll bet it weighed half a pound." He kept tame pigeons which he used to sell to other boys, telling them to keep them shut up for two days, then they would not come back to him. But of course they did come back, and Bill had them to sell again. Someone said "There is not much pay in keeping pigeons, is there, Bill?" He said "No, I have lost money on every pigeon I have sold yet, but it's the quantity I sell where I make my money." When somebody asked if the fat pig he had killed on Monday was as heavy as he thought, Bill said "No, I did not think it would be." One day we were talking about the weather and the hard winters we had known when Bill looked up and said, "I remember one winter we had six weeks frost in February." Another day we were talking about the price of potatoes, and Bill said "I sold Fred Saunders a hundredweight for four shillings and he never paid me for them. If I had known he was not going to pay for them I would have charged him more." Once when we were comparing the price of things, Bill spoke up and said "I remember when bacon was one shilling a loaf." Once he bought some seed potatoes, and asked the seedsman to send them to Bourton-on-the-Water station. Someone asked him if he had got his seed potatoes yet, and he said "No, I've been down to the station twice and they baint there. I be going down again today, and if they baint there I'll send them back."

Next door to me lives Tom Willis. During the First World War he served in the Navy, then he came back and went to work on the roads where he used the old breast plough for trimming the sides. I was talking to him one day when he said "You know, George, I have ploughed the land, the sea and the roads, and now I should like to plough the air in an aeroplane." One day I asked him if he had got his seed potatoes in yet. He said "Yes, but I am not planting so many this time. I only bought half a hundredweight, but when they came they were all big ones so I cut them all in two and made a hundredweight of them, so I suppose I shall have to plant them now I have got them." One day a man working with Tom asked him if he would like a toffee. Tom put it straight into his mouth. The man said "Don't you take the paper off them?" "No," he said, "they last longer with the paper on."

One time I was working with a man from Leafield and he told me his wife was expecting a baby soon. One day he did not come to work, but the next day he came as usual so I said to him "Where did you get to yesterday?" "Oh, the wife has had her baby, and they are both as well as can be expected." I said "That's good. What have you got this time?" "Ah," he said, "you guess." I said, "A boy," but he said no, so I said "A girl?" "Ah," he said, "somebody must have told you." Another man I was working with said "I do like apple dumplings. My mother always makes me one, and when she haven't got any apple she puts a tater in instead, and when it's cooked I throw the tater away and eats the apple dumpling." Then while I was working at Shilton there were two brothers named Timms working on the same job. Across the way was a young woman who tried to attract their attention. One of the brothers went to Burford Fair and met this young woman, and she said to him "Hello, is it you or your brother?" He said "My brother." "Ah," she said, "I thought 'twasn't you." And then there was Jack Westbury's wife who said she was sorry to hear that wages were going up, for when Jack was out of work it would be such a great loss of wages.

There are many members of the Farmer family in Filkins. My great-grandfather who was a builder in Chalford used to come over to the Filkins quarry, and he married Miss Farmer whose father was in charge, and moved to Filkins where our family have been ever since. There are many stories I could tell of Long John Farmer, Fiddler Farmer and his son Salter Farmer, Tiddly John and Donkey John, and I have already mentioned my great-uncle, Job Farmer. But instead I will tell some of the tales told to me and my father by Charles Farmer, my old friend, who died aged seventy-nine in 1956.

Job Cobbett, salt merchant of Lechlade, used to bring salt round to the villages for sale in a small cart drawn by a team of dogs. He travelled from Lechlade to Little Faringdon, Langford, Broadwell and Kencot, and then back to The Lamb Inn at Filkins by midday, where he stayed and had his dinner. Here he unharnessed his dogs and let them run wild around the village to pick up a few scraps of food where they could. People saved bones for them, as they knew the day when the salt man came. When John was ready to start he blew a horn and his dogs came back to him, and he harnessed them up and was soon on his way again. John had his salt sent to him by barge to the Lechlade Wharf, where so many other goods came in before the railway was built.

Many years ago a farmer at Broughton discovered one morning that someone had broken into his house and stolen a cheese and a piece of bacon. Steps were taken to trace the culprit, but without success. Then one morning the carter out on early duty noticed a man near the churchyard gate. Thinking it strange, he watched and saw him go to an old tomb, and lifting the broken top take out the bacon and cheese, cut off what he required, put the rest back and replace the top. The old carter kept the secret and never reported it.

Thomas Clack was known to many as the Farmers' Calendar. He knew the best time to plant almost anything, and his advice was often sought. The school holidays never commenced until he had been consulted as to when the harvest would begin. Though possessing a watch, he was renowned for guessing the right time. He talked a lot about Queen Victoria's Coronation, and also the different wet and dry seasons he remembered.

Years ago a farmer at Oxleaze employed a man as a shepherd. He lived in a house at the top of Filkins in the part which is called The Gardens. The man was efficient at his work and gave the farmer satisfaction, but sometimes there seemed to be a lamb missing. The farmer thought a mistake had been made in counting them, and did not make any bother about it. But the shepherd's children betrayed him. While playing with other children and saying what they liked best to eat, they said they did not like mutton as they had it for every meal, and had plenty up in the attic now. The farmer sent for the constable to search, who found nearly a whole lamb hung on the beam in the attic. The shepherd was instantly dismissed and the punishment might have been severe, but sympathy was shown for the man's wife and children.

One pay night when Farmer Hiett was paying his servants he began to complain of the bad times and said "I can see we shall all finish up in the Workhouse." Fanny Swinford replied "Never mind, master, if we can sit at the same table as you, we shan't hurt."

An old blacksmith at Kencot told me that one day the hounds were meeting at Bradwell Grove, so I thought why not have a day off like the rest. I never did like blacksmithing, so off I went to the meet. Very soon along came the landlord from The Bull Inn on his old cob. He says to me "Come and hold my nag a few minutes. I shan't be long." I thought, now is my chance. No sooner was he gone than I was on the horse's back and away after the hounds. The horse went well and I had three hours good sport. Then I thought I had better make for home, so I got back to The Bull Inn at Filkins, put the horse in the stable and gave him a feed, and went to the back door where I said "I have brought the horse home and give him a feed, and I was to have a pint of ale." I had hardly drunk the ale when I saw the landlord, tired out, coming down the street, so I slipped out of the back door and across the fields to Kencot. I did not call at The Bull Inn for some time after that. When I met the old man he threatened me, but later we both thought it a great joke.

Men used to visit the markets to get a job of driving sheep or cattle home for the farmer who bought them. They were called drovers. A Burford farmer bought some sheep at Lechlade market and asked a drover to drive them home for him. The man started off with them, and had not got very far when he began to think what a long way it was to Burford and back again to Lechlade. So he thought of an idea. He put one of the sheep into a field and left it there, and went on to Burford with the others. When he arrived the farmer asked him if he had them all and he said "No sir, one went lame so I put it in a field. If you will put the pony in the trap I will go back with you and help you load it." The farmer paid him and gave him some food and drink, and then they set off to get the lame sheep. When they got to the field the farmer said "Well, that sheep doesn't look very lame, and the drover said "No sir, not half so lame as I should have been if I had walked back from Burford."

When my father was a boy he went to Langford School. One day news came that the wonderful thrashing machine was down at Lower Farm. At dinner time the children went down to see it and found a large crowd of people with the same interest. As the man started the engine, up went the steam and soot. When some of the men saw the fire in the fire box they shook their heads and said it would never answer, as they pictured fires being started in the rickyards.

Now I have written a few pages of stories told me by my old friend Charles Farmer, and also some of my own memories of Filkins people. We had some very kind ones who were always ready and willing to help those in need. When a baby was born neighbours would volunteer to do washing or look after the other children, and never think of being paid. If a man was ill someone would help do the garden, chop up firewood or look after the livestock if he had any. Then there was the midwife who was also the village nurse. She was paid little, but she never overcharged, although it was her living. I think people helped each other more in the days when I was a boy than they do today. They found pleasure in helping someone without being paid.

I shall end with a poem Charles Farmer told me. It was called "Time".

When I was a child I slept and wept,
Time crept.
When as a youth I laughed and talked

Time walked.
When I became a full grown man
Time ran.
And older as I daily grew
Time flew.
Soon I shall be travelling on,
Time gone.

CHAPTER
EIGHT

First World War

When the 1914 War started there were recruiting meetings held in all the villages round about. At the ones in Filkins the village band played, and an old retired officer would speak. I remember he said that if we joined up the war would be over in six months. We would never have to go to the front, because the Kaiser would pack up when he heard we had such a big army.

Then came Lord Kitchener's appeal for 500,000 men, and I signed up on 20th December 1915. I had to cycle to Witney to sign up, and there were thousands of men waiting in a line. I did not get in until 7 pm. I remember that because I had no lights on my bicycle, but a policeman said it would be all right.

My age group, I was twenty-seven then, was called up on 1st June 1916. I reported to Oxford and joined the Royal Engineers. I was sent to Clipstone Camp near Mansfield where we were innoculated, fitted up with clothes and taught to march. After a month we were sent to Chatham to do our Trade Tests. Then we went to North Wales, to Conway Camp.

We did drill on the promenade at Llandudno, and we

used to march backwards and forwards over Conway suspension bridge. It was August, and hard work marching about on the hot asphalt. Lord French came once to inspect us. I remember we had a half holiday, but you could not leave the camp otherwise.

I passed all my exams in sapping, mining, knots and lashings, demolitions and bridge building, and was waiting to go to the River Conway to do pontoon bridging which was the last thing. Then on Sunday morning notices were put up that every man in the camp was to be on parade at ten o'clock.

As our names were read out we fell out on the left, until every man except the sick was lined up. Rumours started, no one knew what it was all about. Then about five o'clock a long list of all our names went up, and it said "These men will proceed to Kemnel Park on Monday morning at eight o'clock for Infantry training." So away we all went to Kemnel Park where we were attached to the Royal Welch Fusiliers.

Every day we paraded at 6 am. We had physical training till 7 am, then back to camp to shave, clean buttons and boots and get into our equipment. Breakfast at 7.30 am then parade at 8 am for inspection. Then about ten miles route march till dinner time. In the afternoon more drill, lectures on rifles and grenades, etc. After tea at 5 pm the rest of the day was our own, but we could not leave camp without a pass.

This transfer to the Infantry was caused by shortage of soldiers in France, and it caused a lot of trouble when we went to get our pay. All us Royal Engineers were entitled to an extra shilling or so a day because we had passed our trade tests. This meant we Sappers in the Infantry were now drawing more than their sergeants. When we went to get our pay, we did not get the extra. And when we asked about it, they told us we were not entitled to it now we were in the Infantry. But we knew we were, so we called a meeting and agreed not to go on parade the next morning until it was settled. When the Orderly Sergeant came round at 6 am we refused to go on parade. The Captain was sent for. He came out in his night attire and asked us to fall in, and tell him what was the matter. This we did, and he promised to get in touch with the R.E. headquarters at Chatham, and find out if we were entitled to the extra pay. Then he sent us back to our barracks, telling us he would call us out later on. Well, later on he did call us out, and told us we were entitled to the extra money, and that we would get it at the end of the week, with all the back pay. So that settled that. But this made bad feeling between us and the sergeants. They did not like to think we were getting more money than them, and they said they would make us earn it. So they tried to push us around, and some of us were up to thirty-five years old and training with eighteen year olds. This caused a lot of men to fall out, and so trouble started again.

Anyway, we got over that trouble, and on the 18th December we finished our training. Then we got forty-eight hours leave, but that had to include getting home and back as well. From the 300 that went on leave, over 250 were late, and it took a week to try us all. I was forty-eight hours late, and received seven days C.B. and seven days pay stopped. Everybody had about the same punishment, but there were quite a lot who never came back at all. We were on draft now, and not allowed out of camp. We had our Christmas there, and on the 31st December at 6 am we started for France.

We came down south through Birmingham and Oxford to Southampton. We crossed the channel in the night, and arrived at Le Havre on New Year's Day 1917. We got off the boat, marched around the town, and got onto another boat which took us up the river to Rouen. We were a draught of about 250 men, and were transferred to the South Lancs which was a front line battalion. Next morning we paraded for a medical and kit inspection and received rifles, gas helmets and ammunition ready for the front. Then a report came from the M.O. to say two men had measles, so we had to be isolated for fourteen days. At the end of the fourteen days we were split into a lot of different units. I was sent to the 11th South Lancs 30 Division with thirty-four others. We set off for the Arras front, and this is when we saw the first fighting.

From now on we were in and out of the line like the others, moving from one section of the front to another all along the front from the Belgians on our left to the French on our right. I was slightly wounded at the Arras front, and there were a good many near misses, but I managed to get through.

On 21st March 1918 when the Germans made their last big drive I was on the St Quentin front, a part we had taken over from the French. We were in the thick of the fighting and lost a lot of our men and materials. For fourteen days we were all mixed up and did not know where we were, at last the French came up and relieved us and we were sent back for a rest. We marched about a hundred miles in ten days to a village near St Valerie. Here we were not allowed from our billet which was a cowshed and pigsties. We had two clear days here and then had orders to be on parade by 6 pm in full marching order. We marched until ten o'clock to a railway station and mounted the train about twelve o'clock and finally arrived in Belgium at Elverdinge. Our party was about sixty men and we were attached to the R.E.

We helped mine bridges and get guns and materials back over the canal preparing for a retreat as the Germans were advancing on our right. We had a fortnight at this job, and as we had been moving around for about five weeks we had no letters or parcels. Now they began to arrive and we got a bit of news from home.

My son George had been three years old when I joined up. My wife had an allowance of fourteen shillings a week, for herself and the child. She had to pay rent, life insurance (the Foresters' Benefit Society), and everything else. She managed to keep everything going, I do not know how. I got an extra shilling a day as I was a trained engineer, which made 3s.6d. a week to send back to her. She never got it for the first six to seven weeks. I went to see an officer and he sent me to the Quartermaster who said "It's nothing to do with you, it's your wife's money, not yours." I got savage and thought, I wish I could leave the Army. However, my wife went to see Mr Lyons at The Five Alls who was an old army pensioner, and he told her where to write, and £3 came to her the next day.

My wife used to send me a loaf every week sewed up

in calico and I had two loaves one day, about a month old, and when I opened them they were green as grass with mildew, but we shaved them with our jack knives and ate them, as we were very short of food at that time and were glad of anything eatable. When we finished this job a division of Belgiums came and took over this part. As we came out we met them going in. They went over at night and took six hundred prisoners. In the morning the roads were full of prisoners, some wounded and some fed up, and we had to wait for two hours before we could get on the roads to get away, as we were ordered to Kemnel Hill. Here we were in the thick of some fighting. Again, sometimes we were on top of the hill and sometimes the Germans were. After this had quietened down we were sent back to our base at Rouen. Here the 30th Division was mustered and there were less than two thousand of us left. We stayed here for a weekend, had our equipment made up as we had lost a lot of our kit in the retreat, and the division was disbanded and split into reinforcements for other divisions. I and about twenty others were sent to the 55th Division to the 1/4th South Lanes on the La Basse front. This was a pioneer battalion. Here we were mending roads, trench digging, wiring and doing general work in the line.

The Germans blew up a canal bridge one day and they sent us to repair it. There was a nice dug-out and sixteen of us were going to stop in it. The corporal came to the top of our steps and said, "Somebody has to go to mine Chelsea bridge. Swinford, you go and report." "Right ho" I said. He stood there saying, "Here's some sugar and tea and bully beef for you." I heard a German shell coming and I crouched down, it knocked my tin hat over my back. Another chap standing below me got shell-shock. The corporal was lifted right over me and blown all to pieces.

The man with shell-shock needed to go to the dressing station. He was shouting "There's nobody to take me". "Come on, I'll take you," I said, and we started off. He was in a terrible state, he kept getting down on his knees pulling up the stones on the road, and I could hardly get him along. When we got there they asked me if I was all right, and I said "Yes, I'm not hurt." They said "What's the matter with your arm?" and I saw that it was covered with blood and flesh off the corporal. They gave me a cup of milk. My leg felt wet and I wondered if I'd been wounded there, but it was just water running out of my water-bottle where a bit of shrapnel had hit it. When I got back the officer said "Where the hell have you been, Swinford?" and I said "Well, we've lost a corporal for one thing."

A terrible time.

During all this time leave had been cancelled. I had not had any leave from France and it was now July 1918 and I had been out there for thirteen months. One morning on parade our sergeant read out a notice saying, if anyone would like to go to Paris for seven days leave to give their names to him, as there were so many allowed. He asked me if I wanted to go and I told him no, if I had any leave I wanted to go home as I had not had a leave at all from France, and had been out here for fifteen months. He was surprised to hear this and said he would report it at once. We were on night work fixing barbed wire in no man's land at the time. We went up to the line at 8 pm and came back at 4 am. When we got back a messenger came into our billet and asked for me, and told me I was for leave and was to report sick at 8 am, so I had to have a clean up and get ready. I was examined by the doctor and then sent to the headquarters to see the colonel. He said he was very sorry I had not had a leave as my papers had been overlooked, but he would get me away as soon as possible. The next day I was on my way home. When I arrived home I found my allotment in rather a bad state, so I spent most of my time getting it into shape again. We came from France to Folkestone and after my fourteen days leave I went back and found my battalion in the same place, and we carried on as usual.

There was one thing that kept me going, sitting awake hour after hour in a dug-out with a candle, up to your knees in water. We had non-safety matches in those days, and when you were lying on the concrete you would crush the match-box, and in your pocket a match might get alight and burn a hole. So I would go up the line to get German shell cases (dangerous job) and make them into matchbox covers, one for each man in the platoon, with his name on it, thirty-five altogether. I was quite noted for them. I found a saw in a ruined butcher's shop, and I got some files and solder off the Transport chaps. I made one for my wife engraved with a carpenter's punch, sharpened up like a chisel. On one side I showed her in a rocking chair I had made for her saying "I wonder how my dear boy is in France", and on the other side I showed myself in a trench picking the lice out of my shirt, saying "I am all right". I had a block of iron the size of a matchbox to use as a mould, to give me the shape. I made a box for Father which opened and shut, made like a baccy box, and quite a lot of paper knives as well. I used to cut cap badges for different regiments, too. I also made two crosses from a lump of copper I found in a field, soldered on to the base. Then there was the jug I made from a French 75 mm shell case, and the handle from an English shell case.

One day I was sent with others to help repair bridges with some R.E.s, I was working with an R.E. whose name was Burnett. He said to me "Give us a light", so I gave him my matchbox, one that I had made from a shell case for my father and had put his name on it, J. Swinford, Filkins. He looked at it and said, "I suppose this is not in Oxfordshire?" and I said "Yes it is." He said "My brother married a girl from there, her name was Holloway." They kept the post office and of course I knew her quite well. When I went home on leave, I told her and she said "Would you take him a bit of jam and cake?" I said "Certainly, but I cannot guarantee I will see him again." So she said, "If you do not see him before Sunday, eat them yourself." I never did see him again so I had to eat them both. This brother of his came and lived here afterwards. He lived in Bath and when he retired he and his wife settled down in Filkins.

Early in October the Germans started their retreat, and we as pioneers were up with the Infantry repairing roads and bridges that had been blown up by the retreating Germans, so that we could get our transport up. We filled the holes in the road with everything we could lay our hands on — telegraph poles, even pieces of ruined homes. Terrible job, it was, seeing people's things left like that. We pulled one whole cottage down and put it into a hole to fill it up. When we came to the fireplace we found the ornaments that had fallen off the mantelpiece — things people had collected. There were vases and a lovely crucifix, and some candlesticks, and other things. Very pretty they were. We parted them among us, and I said I would like the candlesticks best, so I put them in my pack.

At another home I spotted a little French china cottage, and I thought I should like to take care of it. We had plenty of tobacco at that time, so I filled it up, packed it nice and tight and carried it round in my pack. I managed to get it home without breaking it, and it has been on my mantelpiece ever since. One of the candlesticks got a bit of shrapnel through it, and so did the spare shirt in my pack. It was like a sieve where the shrapnel had been.

On the morning of the Armistice we were in Belgium in a small town called Ath filling up shell-holes. An aeroplane flew low overhead and the pilot waved his handkerchief and said "The War's over." But we weren't quite sure, so we just went on to fill up the next hole. We stopped to let the Artillery go by, and the Captain who was on a big horse shouted "Halt, about turn." Our sergeant asked him "Is the War over?" and he said "Yes." Some of our men pulled their tin hats off and threw them under the wheels, but we were not really excited. It was like silence. You see, for one thing one of the messengers in the Cycle Corps had got killed, and was lying by the side of the road, and we were sent to dig his grave. We said to each other "Bet they are having a good time in London." But we were still there in Belgium, and digging a grave in the last hour of the war. I often think of that incident.

We were just on the outskirts of Ath. We stayed in this place for a few weeks and then we marched on to Brussels. We were billeted in a house with a Belgian family, and we had some new underclothes and a bath and were treated very well, and spent our Christmas here. We had a concert one night in a hall we had taken over, and at the interval our officers threw oranges and apples into the audience and I caught an orange. Sitting behind me was a boy and his older sister, so I gave the boy my orange and I heard her say to him "Say thank you sir", so he said it to me. I said to the girl "You speak English". She said "Yes, my great-grandfather was English, he came to the Battle of Waterloo and stayed here." She gave me an invitation to go to her house, so on Sunday morning I and my pal went and found her house. They made us very welcome and told us their history. We visited them often after this and had some enjoyable evenings with them. He had a grandfather clock in the house and said this clock was in the guardroom at Waterloo, and he showed me the chalk marks where the prisoners marked their seven days or fourteen days off in strokes. The back of the clock was covered with marks like this IIIIIIIIIIIII. He said "My clock would be valuable in England."

We had a lot of invitations out to people's homes while staying in Brussels, and one family asked us to tea and gave us their card, so we went on Sunday. They had a hairdressing business. The man could talk good English, as he said he had been to England in a competition at Crystal Palace several times for hairdressing. They were very busy, so he said his wife would take us out and show us around. She went with us to the picture gallery and museum, and one place she wanted to go to was St Giles Prison where Nurse Cavell was shot. She could not get in without going in with soldiers, so we went and a Belgium guard took us round to the spot where Nurse Cavell stood and was shot. There was a paving stone, and we each one stood on this stone. Then we went down in the garden where there were a lot of graves of the people who had been shot for spying, and Nurse Cavell's grave was there too, but we could not see it for wreaths. I asked the guard if I could have a souvenir and he said yes, so I picked a laurel leaf off one of the wreaths. I have still got it here and I prize it very much. Now we are in January 1919 and hoping to get demobilized and come home.

That was not the end though. The strike was on in England and there were no jobs and hundreds of unemployed. You had to have a letter from your boss offering you a job. My wife was eager to get me home, and as Father was working at Filkins Hall he got Mr Groves to write for me, and I got away. I had an examination to see I was not lousy, got past the doctors, had a bath and a clean shirt. Thousands with no job to go to stayed on there. Eventually I arrived at Chiseldon Camp near Swindon on 30th January 1919, and the next day I had finished with the Army. I had served two years and eight months and come home three times in that period. I think now how lucky I was to get back home with only one slight wound and very little sickness.

I had a week at home, although I was entitled to twenty-eight days furlough. Then I went back to work. One owner of a big house said to me "You would not have missed it for anything would you, my boy?" and I said "My God, I *would*."

Now I can't find another man who has been in any of it with me. It seems I am the only one left.

CHAPTER
NINE

Stone

I would now like to write in more detail about stone, as this is the first thing any visitor to Filkins notices. We have several quarries in the village. I will deal first with two which are on the right hand side of the Barrington Road about a quarter of a mile from the village, called the Longround and the Horsebottom Quarry. This stone is called Forest Marble and contains numerous shells, fossilized wood and bone. Geologists tell me the period of its formation was about thirty million years ago. While digging in the Longround we found a portion of a shark's jaw which is known as the Port Jackson Shark. It swims on the bottom of the sea and scoops up shellfish in its mouth, crushes them, sucks out the goodness and spits out the shells, which we find bedded on the stone in quantities. This portion of jaw I have in the Museum is about three inches by two inches, showing the fossilized bone and the shiny black teeth attached.

In the past the quarries have been worked a lot as there are several acres of old workings from about the fourteenth century to the beginning of the nineteenth century. The last people to work these quarries before we started in 1929 were French prisoners of war from the Battle of Waterloo. I have heard the old men talk of the French prisoners. Some said it was four and some said it was six. Where we started was where the French men left off, and we found several clay pipes, a pickaxe and shovel.

Sir Stafford bought these quarries in 1929 and the next year we started digging there. Since then we have dug 190 thousand slates, eleven thousand cubic yards of building stone and 160 tons of paving stone, besides large quantities of road stones. A small portion of this was sold, but most of it was used locally for building council houses, building the village centre and repairs to farm buildings, St Peters House and the Church of England school at Langford. It is a good general purpose stone, a grey colour, and will stand the weather well. In the quarry one can see the different layers of rock and clay formed when it was under the sea. This stone was all dug by hand as it would spoil too much if dug by machinery. It is very hard work and must have skilled men to sort it while digging and put it in different stacks for different purposes, such as slates, dry-walling building, road and paving.

We have other quarries in the village but they do not produce such good stone, although it is a bit cheaper to dig. It is cream in colour but will not stand the weather unless it is kept dry. One quarry is on the left, opposite the Longround and is called Larklands. There are also quarries at College Farm called White Hill where they used to dig the stone for floors in the houses and barns. This stone is cream in colour and looks nice and clean when washed and finished with skimmed milk which puts a glaze on it. There is still some to be seen in the old cottages and barns today. A family named Farmer used to dig this and work it. They used a donkey to pull it out of the quarry on a truck.

There are also lots of places where they dug stone for road mending. You can see the hollows in the fields where they dug it. This was surface stone and was very rough so not suitable for building except dry-walling. On the side of the roads too they dug stone for mending roads, you can see hollows up the College Road and the Burford Road, used now as tips for rubbish.

In the old days the stone digging was done mostly as piece-work. Men used to contract for the job at so much a yard cube, which meant taking off the top, or ridding as it was called, down to the rock. Then they dug the stone and wheeled it out and stacked it one yard high. A stack ten yards by ten yards and one yard high was a hundred yard cube. The price varied in different quarries, the lowest price I remember was 6¼d per yard. Charles Webb dug them at this price for Mr Hoddinott in Larklands quarry for road mending. The general rule was when stone was wanted for the roads, the road surveyor (Mr Powell was then surveyor) would put up printed notices asking for prices in different quarries, then men would send in their prices and the lowest price was accepted. There was a great competition for this as it was a job in the winter and those days there was not much work about, and it was very hard work to earn ten shillings per week. The stone was hauled to the roadside by contract. This caused competition too, loads were tipped along the side of the road about forty yards apart, then men were contracted to break the stone up at so much a load. They were expected to break them small enough to go through a two inch ring. The price was one shilling per load and there seemed always someone who was willing to do it at that low price as work was so scarce at this time.

Stone chopping or dressing was done piece-work too. It varied in price from one shilling to one and sixpence per yard. It was a good days work to do four yards. It was hard work, I remember when we were doing it for several weeks my arm ached so badly I could not sleep. Banker work involved cutting and dressing the stone for quoins and window mullions, etc.

Masons were journeymen travelling from one job to another, sometimes walking long distances or lodging near the job. I have heard my father say how he walked from Filkins to Tetbury at weekends when the Church was built. He worked to 1 pm on Saturday, walked home, did a bit of gardening and started back to Tetbury on Sunday night as the bells were ringing for the 6 pm service at Church. He was there ready to start work at 6 am on Monday morning. He walked to Burford grammar school and back every day for three months, getting there in the morning by 6 am and working to 7 pm at night, then walking home five miles. The journeyman did a lot of walking so I had to when I started work. Then the bicycle came and the old journeyman said it was the best friend the workers ever had. Wages were sixpence per hour in about 1900 and rose to sevenpence per hour by the time the 1914–18 war started. After the war it went up to 1s.11d. per hour. Men joined the unions and got the eight hour day. Then the slump came and there was unemployment in the building trades and the wages dropped to 1s.4d. per hour in about five weeks. Nobody could do anything about it, and it remained about this level until the last war started. The men were wanted badly for building aerodromes, and wages went steadily up again, and as there has usually been plenty of work since the war, wages have gradually increased. I have given these figures as a local guide, in towns they varied in different districts.

When I worked with my father doing dry-stone walling before the Second World War we were paid 3s.6d. per chain of twenty-two yards.

As I have said, masons in country districts helped to make the stone slates and put them on, but there were other men called slaters and plasterers who kept to their trades. The Filkins slates were reckoned to be some of the best slates, as they were what we call presents. That means they did not have to be left out over winter to be split by the frost like the Stonesfield slates. They come from the Quarry in thin slabs ready for making up and the frost does not affect them. We sometimes get some large ones out, the largest I remember was nine feet by six feet and it was only about one inch thick. These large ones were used mostly on pigsties or buildings of this sort. Some large thick ones called slats were stood upright in the ground and used as fences round some of the cottage gardens. You can see some by the bowling green. Slats were used as fences on each side of footpaths, to keep the sheep in and divide up the fields, sometimes instead of dry-stone walls. The path from Filkins to Broadwell across the fields had slats on each side, with special stones where the coffin-bearers rested the coffin on the journey to the churchyard, when we had no church of our own at Filkins.

The slates were made by piece-work. The price paid in 1935 was £2 15s. per thousand, and if we sold any the price was £6 10s. per thousand. The way we count the slates is different from other districts. We count every slate over fourteen inches from hole to tail as five and all under fourteen inches are counted as one. We generally made up a thousand slates with 120 large ones and 400 small ones. We used to reckon that 700 would cover one square (or 100 square feet). It was a craftsman's job making these slates as it was easy to break them when nearly finished. Picking the hole was a difficult job and of course it wanted some good tools to stand up to this very hard stone. In the old days these slates were hung on lathes with wooden pegs driven through the hole in the slate. The best wood for those pegs was yew, the old men used to say they will last for ever. Now they are generally nailed on with galvanized nails. It is also a craftsman's job putting these slates on. We still use the old slate rule that originated from the Romans with the Roman figures. I have my grandfather's rule in the Museum.

The swept valleys of the roofs that were done without lead was a craftsman's job too, for to keep out the rain in a valley is difficult without lead or zinc. Stone slating is hard to explain in writing, and I am sorry to say there are very few good slaters about these days. My grandfather on my mother's side, George Willis, was a slater and plasterer, and he was also a lath renderer. The laths were made from oak, poplar, and Scotch fir. The thinnest laths were used for hanging the slates on the roofs. The timber used for laths had to be free from knots, as they would stop the rendering and make a lot of waste. They used a special tool, like the hurdle-makers use for splitting the poles for hurdles.

About 1952 I made ten thousand slates for Mr J. Cripps, and I wondered then whether any more would be dug. I was retiring and there was no sign of getting the right sort of labour.

Of course there were still quarries being worked in the Cotswolds for freestone, that is blocks of stone for carving and making window mullions and fireplaces, etc., and rubble stone for walling, but there was hardly any stone thin enough for roofing dug after we finished.

A lot of worn-out stone roofs have been replaced by imitation stone slates made of concrete. My nephew Mervyn made them for years, since he was helping build the new council houses. They ran out of the proper slate so Mervyn and my brother Joe tried their hand at making some concrete ones and have carried on ever since.

But when some slate has been wanted for a job, the builder has to look around for second-hand ones off a building being taken down. People might think it funny reusing an old roof, but a lot of old cottages have been pulled down since I can remember and of course a lot have been built, also some old farm buildings which were in bad repair have been taken down, and a lot of the stone has been reused on other buildings. The year I left school, 1899, Mr Fox of Bradwell built a reading room and let it to the village at a shilling a year. It was built opposite the church where a row of old cottages had previously stood. I expect the stone was used somewhere else.

Sir Stafford Cripps' house, Goodfellows, was always known as Moat Farm from when I was a boy because of the moat all round the house, fed from a spring in the grounds. The centre part of the house was seventeenth century, but from the old stone we found in the buildings there must have been a house before. We found old carved stone and moulded stone probably from the fourteenth century, when I was working for Sir Stafford in the 1930s.

The new wing on the south-west we built of the stone from an old barn up the College Road, called Dees barn. The freestone windows, etc. came from Farmington. We also built the fire bridges and the terrace on the north side, partly from stone from old buildings on the farm.

So long as stone is used, whether new or reused, and the style of building is the same, new buildings quickly weather down and fit into the village. For instance, St Peters House where Mr J. Cripps lived, looks like an old Cotswold house, but was only built in 1930 for Mr A. S. C. Austin, the vicar, to retire to. He retired in 1942 and owing to the War he sold it to Mr Cripps and went to live in Eastbourne. Mr C. Johnston was the architect and my brother Joe Swinford was builder. And of course Filkins Hall was only built in 1912. The new vicarage is all in stone too and was built in 1950. Here are the accounts: (see page 160).

The old vicarage was Green Dragon House next to the church.

	£	s.	d.
Messrs. Groves Builders	4865	18	2
Development charge	100	0	0
Architect Fees	271	0	0
Quantity Surveyors fees	31	0	0
Diocesan Registrars Fees		17	0
Special ex water supply & drive	54	8	6
	5479	7	7

	£	s.	d.
Sale of old vicarage	2250	0	0
Interest on sale proceeds	25	15	11
Local accounts	906	8	10
Interest on local accounts	31	14	4
Diocesan expenses fund —			
Broughton Rectory Diocesan gt	25	0	0
Diocesan payment legal charges	36	17	0
Church Commissioners grant	250	0	0
Loan from Commissioners	1026	0	0
	5479	7	7

Things have changed a bit now. Builders still use stone but also artificial stone and concrete more and more. However, the old quarry at Horsebottom has lately been opened up again by Mr Seymour Aitkin, and even though they use machines to dig and trim the slates it is nice to know that Filkins stone is again being quarried.

CHAPTER
TEN

Later Life

I came back from the First World War in 1919 and started work for Mr Groves again and was on regularly for him until September 1925. My daughter Freda was born on 30th March 1920. We were still living opposite The Five Alls then. We had a terrible flood the week she was born and Broughton was flooded two feet deep in some places, cars were stranded and had to be pulled out with horses. My mother died on 22nd February 1923 aged fifty-five years.

In 1925 I had a job with Mr Groves at a place called Chelworth Manor near Crudwell in Wiltshire, when Sir Stafford Cripps sent down his chauffeur to where I was lodging as he wanted to see me. I was to meet him on Saturday night at Goodfellows, where he had come in 1920.

When I went to see him, he said, "I have had a very good account of you and I should like to have a man I can trust to do some stonewalling, and some work indoors with wood, and also on the estate. Would you care for the job?" I said, "I have a very interesting job and good wage at present." Sir Stafford said, "I would pay the same and give you better conditions. Go home and talk to your wife about it." My wife wanted me to be close to home, as I was away from home all the winter in lodgings, so she said, "Yes, I would like it better for you to stop here."

Sir Stafford wrote out the conditions and on 25th September 1925 I started work for him. The first thing was to make a workshop, and then I repaired some furniture and made some new. Although I was a mason I was always very keen on woodwork and have often done a bit of carving. Then I started to repair the buildings and had a labourer to help, and got on very nicely. Then more work came along and I took on more men, and at one time I had thirty-one men under me.

In 1928 Sir Stafford bought Manor Farm, and I was doing some work in Goodfellows garden when he and Lady Cripps came to me and said they had not had time to look round the farm buildings or cottages yet, so they would like to go with me and see what they were like. We found it all in a very bad state. In the afternoon they both came out to me and said, "George we have been talking about the farm cottages and we don't think it right for you to be building us a pleasure garden when those people are living in such bad conditions. Leave this job at once and go and do what you think is best to improve their conditions." We left off the garden job and started on the cottages the next day and made a lot of improvements.

About 1928 the Rural District Council was talking of building new cottages in the village. They proposed to build them in bricks which Sir Stafford objected to very much. He thought Cotswold villages should be kept stone. Now on the Manor farmland there were three quarries which had been closed for over a hundred years but Sir Stafford thought might be opened up again for stone.

In December we sent three men to take off the top and see what we could find. It was very frosty and cold at this time and Sir Stafford was very concerned about the men not having a fire to sit by at mealtimes, so he told me to make a stove from a large oil drum. This I did, and he carried a sack of coke and I carried the stove up to the quarries. We found plenty of good stone with slates and paving.

One day Sir Stafford said to me, "I am having some members of the RDC down and we are going to have a talk about these new houses. If they would allow me to build them in stone would you run the job?" I said I would. We had the meeting in Sir Stafford's study and Lady Cripps joined us, and after a long discussion Sir Stafford offered to build them in stone and pay the extra cost of building, if he could have his own architect and own design, and when finished he would hand them over to the council. The council agreed to this if they approved of the design, site, etc. So when the plans and the site were settled we started to build the first four cottages which you see near the village centre. At this time work was scarce and it was a good job for the village as we employed men digging stone and slate, while the masons made them ready for the building. We started building in September 1929. Sir Stafford employed Mr C. Johnson to do the clerical work which helped me a lot. In May 1930 we finished these cottages and they were opened by Mr Greenwood MP who was then Minister of Health in the Labour Government.

About this time Langford school was built and our men dug the stone which Sir Stafford and Lady Cripps gave as their contribution. Sir Stafford was always concerned about the conditions of the working class and he told me to pay the men the union rate of wages, he also had ideas of a village centre which he talked to me of quite a lot. Also about this time a young architect came from Canada who was a friend of his relations, and he came and stayed at Goodfellows for a few days. He was very interested in our Cotswold buildings, but he did not know much about stonework. One day Sir Stafford asked me if I would take this man, whose name was Stanley Roth, on a tour and show him some of the noted buildings in the district, so I had a good day out with him in the car and we both enjoyed it very much. He decided to try his hand and get some work here and stay in England, so Sir Stafford offered him his first job to design the village centre. We started to get stone and slates from the quarries and early in 1935 we started to build the village centre, and at Christmas 1935 it was opened by Mr George Lansbury MP. Another idea of Sir Stafford's was to build a swimming pool, and this was done the following year, so now we had the hot baths and a swimming pool. I had the first hot bath ticket, and I was the first to enter the pool when it was finished.

When the village centre was built, Sir Stafford Cripps suggested that the plot in front of the centre should be made into a bowling green and he asked me to approach the men and see what they thought about it. He said he would help us if we would do some of the work ourselves, so we agreed to this, and I and a few helpers dug it over twice, levelled it and raked the stones off and got it ready for turfing. This we did in our spare time. The question then was where to get the turf from and I remembered at Lodge Park they had laid down some golf courses in about 1909 and formed a golf club there (this club lasted only a few years). I had heard of people getting turf from there for lawns and that it was good turf, so I told Sir Stafford and he wrote a letter to Lord Sherborne and asked if we could have some. Lord Sherborne wrote back and said he would be pleased to give us the turf if we would cut it, and we could have what we wanted. Albert Tinson was taken over in the morning by lorry and fetched back at night with a load of turf, and next day we volunteers laid it down. This is the story of how we got our Bowling Green. The next year, 1937, we started playing and had a few matches. Fifield near the Stow Road was the first team we played and we have had the pleasure of playing them every year since and have always had some nice games with them. We have had some very nice outings with the bowls club and some good games. We used to visit the Oxford bowls clubs, and twice we went to Brighton to play a Preston Park club, had a good day at Cirencester and Swindon, and also played the local teams. But now there seems little interest in the club, we have very few members and nobody seems to want to take any responsibility. It is a job to get a secretary or captain. T. Allan was secretary for several years and a good job he made of it until he died, which was a great loss to the club. David Bumford was a good captain, he kept us together, we missed him very much when he went away.

Sir Stafford had another idea of building a playing ground for the children, he thought it would keep the children off the roads, so this scheme was worked out and we started to prepare the land, build the walls around and do the drains. Then we had a firm come along and fix the swings, the chute, etc., and the asphalt was laid. In the playing ground a well was bored for water to supply the village, the centre and swimming pool. Plenty of water was found about ninety feet down. The playing ground was given to the children of the parish in memory of Sir Stafford's son John's marriage to Ursula Davies, 29th December 1930.

Now we had a village centre which consisted of a caretaker's flat, three hot baths, a doctor's surgery, two changing rooms, a swimming pool, a children's playing ground and a bowling green. We also built two small cottages for older people which were handed to the Witney RDC. When the work was finished it was given to the parish in the care of the Parish Council. On the rain-water heads there is a monogram which stands for

Isobel and Stafford Cripps
Filkins Parish Council. 1935

As I have mentioned Sir Stafford also helped the church, in that he gave the black and white marble tiles in the Chancel.

That reminds me of the war memorial right outside the

church. Years before, about 1919, a meeting was called to consider building a war memorial. Mr S. Goodenough said he would give a piece of land to build it on so this was agreed to, and a design made for the cross. When it was built from subscriptions collected in the parish, Mr C. Goodenough claimed he had the right to make the conditions and rules for the memorial, as it was built on his land. He said the land had not been properly handed over to the parish, and he had the right to do what he liked. One of the rules was that no religious meeting was to be held inside the boundary walls. This caused some friction between him and our vicar Mr Austin. So on Armistice Day, meetings were held outside in the road.

Up until 1930 I had been living for fifteen years in a small cottage with no garden, with the allotment a long way off. That year, Sir Stafford bought the Maltster's Cottage near the town pool bridge and we restored it. He said "We don't want just anybody coming to live here," so I moved in. Then on Christmas morning 1931 I was lighting the fire when Sir Stafford came in. He said "I have a little present for you," and handed me the papers of the house. He gave it to me for life, a very good present I thought, and I am pleased to say I am still enjoying his generosity.

We called the house "Cotswold", and a lot of noted people have visited me here during Sir Stafford's political life. They included Mr H. Morrison, Mr C. Lansbury, Mr A. Greenwood, Mr C. Attlee, Dr Addison, Pandit Nehru and many more. These men were on a visit to Goodfellows and Sir Stafford Cripps used to bring them round to see me and have a chat. I still show visitors the chair I carved which Pandit Nehru sat on in my cottage.

Those years were the best years of my working life. Up until I worked for Sir Stafford jobs had sometimes been few and far between. You worked for a week or two at a time, little short jobs not worth talking about for a shilling or two. We would do eight chains of dry stonewalling with a three mile walk each way. I don't believe there was ever such a thing as "the good old times". Most things are better now. I like the old ways, working and building in stone, but I remember times when there wasn't any work at all. Before the Second World War I always had work, and I sat for twenty-nine years on the Parish Council, just as my father had done for thirty-one years.

There were bad times too though. We were only in Cotswold two years when my wife became ill, in 1933. Lady Cripps was very good. She said, "Anything you want, let me know and I will get it." She had paid into the Nursing Association where you could ask for nurses day and night. Lady Cripps supplied both and had them to live in her house for five or six weeks. Then my wife went to the Radcliffe Infirmary in Oxford where she died on 9th August 1933. The doctor's bill was an expensive job, but Lady Cripps paid it all, although I told her I had saved £20.

I felt I wanted to do something for her. She had a four-poster bed with a very old mattress and she said, "George, we must get a new mattress." I measured it up and we got it made at Heals. It was very nice and suited the bed very well. Then she said, "George I don't like the bedstead, I think I'll get a new one altogether."

Now my wife had gone I was on my own. I sat and thought about it, and wondered if I could make a bedstead. I drew it out and thought to myself I could make a nice one. I started making it while Lady Cripps was in London and worked on it every night, carving by the fireside, right through the winter until Easter. When she saw it she said "I know what you have put into it. You were thinking about your wife." The bedstead was made of oak. As I have said, my wife died in 1933 and my wife's sister Miss Sowden came to live with me as my housekeeper. My daughter who was thirteen years old then was at Burford grammar school and my son was in the Air Force and was going abroad. He came home in 1938 and was married soon after at Bristol. In 1945 my daughter married a US Airman and went to America the following year. At this time Miss Sowden was not in very good health and was over seventy years old. She told me she could not carry on much longer, so this made me wonder what I should do, as my son was living in Bristol and my daughter was in America.

I had been talking to another lady, Lily Clapton, who lived across the way. We were just friends. She was nursing her father, and I used to go and sit with her. Then he died and she started taking in lodgers. She told me it was going to cost £300 to put in sanitary arrangements, and I told her I would be on my own soon. So she said, "Well, couldn't we get married?" So we did, on 14th July 1945. Miss Sowden went to live with her younger sister at Redhill.

Meanwhile I continued working for Sir Stafford after the Village Centre was finished. We always had a few jobs looked out for us to go on with, and one of the things we did was to put the new wing on the house at Goodfellows. This was quite a big job. The large room was about eighteen feet by thirty-five feet, and panelled in oak with an oak floor, it was called the library. The oak has been taken out now as it was not damaged by the fire. We also put new roofs on other parts of the house, the old pigeon house we restored with a new roof. A barn and the old cart shed had a new roof too, and we built a new cart shed. Goodfellows cottage we restored, and the moat cottages including the one where I live now. We also built five bridges, the terrace and garden wall in Goodfellows gardens, and made the new drive and hard tennis court and paved the courtyard, and we built the two summer houses in the garden and did lots of other small jobs.

About 1936 the WRDC decided to build twelve more council houses in place of the twelve in Rouses Lane which were in bad repair and not considered to be worth restoring, so they reported it to Sir Stafford and asked him if he would do them as he had done the first four. He came to me and said would I do the job and I said I would, so he got Mr Stanley Roth to get out some plans. The WRDC paid Sir Stafford the price of a brick cottage and he paid the extra cost himself. We got extra men up at the quarry and started to get out the stone and slate and then we started on the building. We finished these cottages in 1938 and then we started repairing the farm buildings. We put on new roofs to the stables and the large barn. Then in 1939 the farm changed hands and Mr Saunders left and Mr V. Arkell came and took over. As he was a hunting man he wanted some stables for his hunters, so we built them near the farmhouse, also a garage.

Sir Stafford had told me months earlier that war was coming, although nobody else seemed to think so. A year before he had been in America, China and Japan. I said, "Do you really think so?" and he said, "Yes, I can't see anything that can stop it." He got all the men together for a meeting, and told them, "Don't start any more work, just put the roof back on the barn, and keep everything going." I remember the barn is twenty-two yards by seven yards — and all the roof timber cost £110. He ploughed up a big field near Goodfellows for anyone who wanted to grow food.

About this time Sir Stafford bought a smaller house at Far Oakridge, near Stroud. As he was closing down Goodfellows and going to Russia this meant that all the staff had to leave, but he asked me if I would go down to Far Oakridge and do some work there and get it ready for his family to make their home for the time being. This I did, then I finished working for him. I finished in rather a sad way as I was taken ill just before the job was finished. I knew they wanted to get in the house, so I asked them to get someone to take charge of the job and finish it. I did not feel well, winter was near and I had been sleeping over the garage and not having proper meals and working long days to get the work done, labour being very scarce at the time. The house was finished and the family moved in.

Sir Stafford's son John Cripps came and lived at Goodfellows then, and cultivated the gardens as market gardener, he also had evacuees from a Bristol school, young children from two to five years old with their nurses and teachers. When the bombing ceased at Bristol the children and nurses went back, and the Land Army took over the house as a hostel for girls. In February 1947 the house caught fire and was almost destroyed. I shall never forget that night. I was gone to bed and about 11.30 pm Mrs Liberty came and knocked at my door and shouted, "Oh do come at once, the hostel is on fire and some of the girls are trapped!" This was the coldest night of the worst winter in memory. I ran down to the house through the snow and I saw the girls jumping out of the windows in a panic, one jumped from the top of the new wing three storeys high, so I went to her and she was unconscious. I thought she was dead. There were two more girls on the roof shouting and saying they were going to jump, but I persuaded them not to, and we would get them down safe. Then Mr John Cripps came and we found a ladder and I went up and got them safe, and we got all the girls up to Mrs Liberty's house. I think there were seventeen or twenty girls altogether. By this time more men arrived, including A. Puffitt, W. Merchant, and the policeman, Mr Nash. The girl that jumped and was unconscious started shouting, so we wrapped her up in our coats and carried her into the drive where we got an ambulance and sent her to the Radcliffe Infirmary. She was badly hurt as she broke her thigh and pelvis, but she got better and came to see me afterwards when she was well enough.

Luckily this was the only serious accident, some of the others cut their arms and knees but nothing more serious. The girls lost all their belongings including their clothes, so the neighbours found them clothes, and gave them a home until they found them another hostel to go to. We had five fire brigades, but although we had plenty of water the roads were so bad with frozen snow they had a job to get here, and the fire had such a hold before they arrived. It was terribly cold and froze very sharp, and to see the flames inside the house and the icicles six feet long hanging down the walls outside was a picture I shall never forget. The firemen's coats were frozen stiff and the hose pipes froze if they stopped using them for a few minutes, and some of the hose pipes laid in the drive froze solid like scaffold poles for a month after the fire. A small portion of the north end was not burnt too badly, and Mr John Cripps made this part into a cottage for the gardener Mr Cox, who was cultivating the garden as a market garden. Other parts have been pulled down as it was not safe.

When the War started I was appointed billeting officer for Filkins and Broughton, and since I had finished work for Sir Stafford I went to work for my brother Joe for a few months. There was still work of a kind. The Government went on putting up pylons, and there was plenty of digging. Not too bad, as I kept my eyes open and found a great many fossils.

There was work particularly at Eynsham. My brother and I were digging big holes by the river. A really nasty job it was, twenty feet into the water. Nobody else wanted to do the worst jobs down the holes, so eventually I said, "Why am *I* doing it? What about some other chaps working with water up to their knees?" At last I packed up and went to work on an aerodrome at Southrop, bricklaying. I got six shillings a week for riding money, as it was over four miles from my home. I was entitled to that, belonging to the union. The boss said, "How do you know it's over four miles?" So I went with him in the car to measure. I didn't take him the shortest way, but just round about a little bit, by The Lamb. He said: "Goodness gracious, it's all of *five* miles!" and I said "Yes, I told you it was over four miles." One day he saw Sir Stafford's board in the village centre at Filkins with my name on it, and he said "George, you should have a better job. Come and see me in the office. I want you to start a new site on Monday. You can go up two pence an hour."

It seemed there was practically no building going on anywhere. Only London was being repaired. In Filkins one new building was in hand, the new vicarage next door to my present house, but I didn't feel I really wanted to do it at sixty-five. I felt like packing up. But the foreman was an old pal of mine, and he said "Come on, George, you'll never get a job nearer home. There's the roof to put on and no slater around, not one. Come on, now, only six weeks to put the slates on." So I did.

After the War, and of course I'd married Lily by then, we had a very nice happy life. We went to America to see my daughter, Freda. We also went to Paris, as they wanted me to see if there was any Cotswold stone in Chartres Cathedral. There wasn't. The last two years together I didn't do much work except at home.

We always had plenty of firewood. Lily was a good housekeeper and cook, and played the organ in chapel. She spent hours on it.

We were always having visitors, and went on picnics and outings. I've got poems somewhere written by visitors saying what a nice time they had with Lily and me at "Cotswold". By this time I had really retired, but there always seemed to be one last job.

One day Mr John Cripps came to me and said the RDC had bought the Gassons, and were going to build about twenty cottages there and they would like to build them in stone, but the job was to get anybody to dig the stone. He asked my opinion about it, so I promised to try and get someone, and said I would go and help. I managed to get two men and we started to dig the stone. We dug enough to build eight cottages, the contractor was Sparks Brothers of Lechlade, and these were finished about 1950. About 1953 the council agreed to build six more, and as they could not get anybody local to dig the stone they had to get them from White Hill near Burford. My brother Joe was the contractor and I chopped most of the stone for him. They were finished in 1955.

In 1952 my brother Joe built a new home for my son George Swinford called Stonehouse. The wall stone came from White Hill, Burford, the freestone from Farmington. The three carvings, the Shepherd, the Mason and the RAF Albatross, I carved for my son. I also chopped most of the wall stone and helped build it. The land where this is built belonged to the old Fox Inn close by.

A new house was built opposite the school for the doctor. It was built in stone from White Hill, Burford.

I chopped most of the wall stones and my brother Joe was the contractor. This house was built in 1956.

Lily and I had a long time together, and as I said, a happy one, but then she got shingles, and her tummy went wrong. I said, "Lily, try and eat." But she said, "If I can't, I can't." I think she wanted to go. She was at the end of her tether, it had all got too much.

I wrote down most of my history of Filkins in 1958, but I am still here thirty years later. Now I'm on my own I often think about my father and the things we used to do together, and I keep remembering something else about Filkins I thought I'd long forgotten.

Now I'm in my nineties I can't do with my hands what I used to. There was a pear tree I drew three years ago, and I got my tools out. I was going to have my bench indoors by the fire and carve it. But I couldn't see the pencil line. I can hardly believe it. But I can still get around the village, and people bring old bits and pieces for the Museum, or just for me to have a look at. They ask how I've lived so long. I think its partly having good habits. I like gardening, and I still get out a good bit in mine, and keep to the old ways, such as you put your kidney beans in on 12th March — Stow Fair day. On Lechlade Fair Day, 9th September, you plant out your cabbages so that you get them for Whitsun. You put your broad beans in in the second week in November. It won't do in some places, but this is Filkins, and those are the dates for Filkins.

Another thing is that I was a staunch teetotaller for thirty years. When I was in the Army and they gave out the rum allowance, I had Oxo cubes, or I might change it with another man for fruit or cake. I gave up smoking when I was fifty-two. This is how it happened. One day my pipe and baccy fell into the fireplace. I stooped down and picked it up and it fell out of my hand again, so as it had happened twice, I said "Dang it! Let it stay there!" And it did. My father gave up smoking at seventy, but he always kept his pipe in his pocket where he could feel it. I was a good athlete too. If you watch football today on the television they are all half asleep.

CHAPTER
ELEVEN

The Museum

I will end my history with a description of the village Museum. I collected most of the things in it and often show visitors round. I'll pick up one of my old mason's tools, or my grandmother's spice box, or one of my mother's rag rugs, and I can see the old times so clearly. Everything has its tale.

As I have mentioned more than once, I was always interested in old relics. As I worked on buildings all my life, digging foundations and drains and levelling sites, I had plenty of opportunity for finding things, as well as an eye for seeing them and a good idea what they were. A lot of things have been found and thrown away again, as the finder did not know what they were. When I find anything interesting I always think I can see the man who made it or used it, and what a difference today with our new designs from what it was then.

When I started work for Sir Stafford Cripps I looked out for anything interesting, and anything worth keeping I used to clean and keep on a shelf in my workshop. For instance one of the first things in my collection was a little donkey shoe which I found when we were digging out the moat at Moat Farm. I began to get quite a collection, and one day Sir Stafford was in my workshop and noticed it. He said, "I am glad you are keeping these things, George. It would be a good idea if we could start a museum, so take care of it all and if we can see a suitable building we will start." After that whenever he came home he would come to the shop to see what else I had found.

Then I heard that an old cottage was for sale on the corner of Rouses Lane. It had once been two cottages. The one on the corner of the lane was where the first Primitive Methodist meetings were held. Later it was made into a stable and coach house for Mr Jesse Farmer's horse and carrier's cart. The other cottage was thatched and one of the oldest buildings in Filkins. Adjoining was the village lock-up or prison which was used up to 1840. The prisoners were shut up for the night, generally for being drunk and quarrelling, and the next day they had to walk five miles to Burford to the police station with the village constable. My grandmother told me she remembered men being shut up there and their wives would go and give them beer in a teapot through the iron bars in the door.

When I told Sir Stafford he said the cottage would do for a museum and that he would buy it, which he did. He then started to make cases to put the exhibits in. I told people in the village what we were doing and asked them if they had anything suitable to let me have it. We soon began to get a lot of things together, and on the 20th May 1931 it was officially opened by Mr Herbert Morrison who was then the Minister of Transport in the Labour Government. From then on I kept collecting, and people brought things along, and we soon had our first place full. We had a notice on the door which read, "The object of this Museum is to preserve objects of common use which are of considerable age, remains of early times, Roman, etc., found in and around the neighbourhood."

We were getting so much that it needed to be catalogued, and Miss Gwendolene Hill who was Sir Stafford's secretary helped me to do this. She spent a lot of her spare time helping and sending articles to the Ashmolean Museum in Oxford to be identified.

Then in 1939 war broke out, and the Home Guard was formed, and they wanted a building for their headquarters. So they took over the old thatched cottage, and that meant all our things had to be taken out and put into the other cottage, and kept locked up until after the War finished.

When it was over I wondered if it was worth while to start it going again. I saw Mr John Cripps and had a talk with him and he said he would like to see it open again. So I sorted everything out and cleaned it up. The thatch of the old cottage was very bad, and the rain had come through and the timber was rotten, so Mr Cripps asked me to put a new stone slate roof on. So I lowered the side walls and put the new roof on, and Mr Cripps paid for it. Luckily the old stone staircase was left and the fireplace with the chimney corner was not damaged, but the old bedroom floor had been taken out.

In 1951 after the new roof was on, we reopened and we now have it in very good order again, and I am still collecting. We charge sixpence entry fee which I use for buying articles of interest and for cleaning materials. Mr Cripps pays the rates and the electric light bill. The Museum is always open to visitors if they collect the key from me, and I generally go in with them to explain things. Visitors who are interested in this folklore history can spend two or three pleasant hours there.

Now we will go on an imaginary tour, and I will show you my collection just as I have to many visitors. We will start in the room which was once the thatched cottage.

These are Dutch Ovens, which everyone used when I was a boy. You put the bacon on top and a piece of toast in the bottom so that the fat dropped onto it. The tinsmith made them, and you would tell him what size you wanted it to be, to suit you.

These two mugs were used in the pubs before they had glasses. One has VR on it and other GR. They are made from what we called Bush china, and the design has a special varnish. One came from The Lamb Inn, and this jug too. This was called a beer slipper. You filled it with beer, added ginger and other spices and put it in the ashes to hot up.

This is a wooden Victorian pint measure for peas or oatmeal, and this is a quart measure. The crown was first on the top, then someone had the idea of cutting the top off and putting in a false bottom, and so the crown was stamped underneath. Quite a dodge.

This mixing bowl was made of elm. Now we've lost the elms. These barrels were used in the fields for beer and cider. The men brought them home at night and someone filled them up and laid them out on the wall ready to be picked up next morning. They hold a gallon. You might think this was quite a lot for a man to drink in a day, but they worked very long hours and it was thirsty work doing everything in the fields by hand. This is a cow's horn cup — quite common for drinking out of before there was a lot of pottery or china around.

These are horn scoops and spoons — this one's for flour. I always liked it. Made of cow's horn — beautiful job. Now this is something you might think was an apple-corer, but it's not — it's an apple scoop made of sheep's bone. My grandmother used it to eat an apple when she no longer had any teeth. Here are some basting needles, and this is a lark toaster. You hung four larks on the little hooks and cooked them back and front, turning them, then put them on the table with the juice.

Here's a lemon squeezer made of wood, sometimes ebony, and here are some scales, also wood. This mincer and this sausage machine were made by hand. They thought a lot of it so they put a beautiful lock on it. I like it because it was all made by hand. And this is a machine for stoning raisins. You cut them with scissors and put them in water, then into the machine and turned the handles and the stones came out at the bottom. We would sit round the table and stone raisins for the plum pudding, and Mother said not to eat them, but you always popped one in on the quiet. And here's a grater for nutmeg, cloves and peppercorns. My grandmother's spice box still smells of spice. She died in 1897.

This is a salamander for griddle cakes, and this is a biscuit mould. This wooden butter dish held half a pound. You had smaller ones for parties. And these are the butter pats. These are choppers for parsley and mint sauce. They were made by the blacksmith and cost about twopence. And this was William Morris's coffee mill.

Here are a colander and vegetable dish, made at Leafield pottery in 1860. This is a dish for beer and cider, and this chamber pot has been photographed a good many times. This collection of Roman pottery was found at Lechlade. This is a fireclay ball used when doing the washing. You heated it up in the fire and then put it into the water to warm it up.

Here is a knife used to carve at the dinner for Queen Victoria's Coronation. Lovely to handle. You always took your own knife to a feast. These two knives are venison carvers, with ivory handles. You didn't have forks often.

This clothes basket on three wheels was for pushing the babies out, two at a time. (You remember I told you how we lost three babies through vaccination and I pushed them out with scabs on them.) This handmade basket was for keeping clothes and instruments for the baby in, and this is the midwife's basket. I came along in that. Old Mrs Ayer the midwife lived by the church at Kencot. She came when my brothers and sisters were born. Sometimes when it was dark I would walk back with her. This baby's bottle is made of countryside china. The next one was glass with a rubber teat and was made to lie in the pram. "The Watchful Mother's Feeding Bottle" is printed on it. These babies' boots cost 2s.11d. The leather is still soft. You used this button hook to do them up.

Here are some of our iron hoops. The girls had wooden ones. We would meet at The Lamb and pick up sides, and the game was to get down to the bridge and back again first, boys against girls. Here are some old skates which were never much good as you couldn't keep them on your feet. We went skating on the Moors, by the brook. This pencil case was mine when I went to school, and this is my old slate. When my sister who, was the eldest, got to school she would give me a bit of chalk to use, but I had to give it back at dinner time. These pencils were made of graphite and were very precious. This penknife was for cutting a quill for a pen — a proper *pen* knife. These balances for sovereigns and half sovereigns are stamped with a crown — a real Government job. And here is my old penny whistle.

Here is a collection of all sorts of things to do with dress. A lot of ladies' shoes — suede ones needing buttonhooks. You used these pattens in the dairy, so as not to get your feet wet. When you went to church you took them off in the porch. My grandmother's pattens were made of wood and iron. Ladies wore these overshoes when they went to a dance. This hook was used for putting on your jack boots. This is a gentleman's top hat stretcher, and this is a hat measurer. These carriers were used to clip onto the bottom of a lady's dress to hold it up out of the mud. Here is her purse, made of silver mesh, and here are her steel beads — Victorian. And here are some side combs which you put through your bun of hair. My Mother had one. This gentleman's wig stand and wig curlers are much older. Also this snuff box. It works like bellows.

My father's uncle put the initials J.S. on this walking stick for my father. I made one and put a hole through it to hang my keys on.

Here is one of Mother's rag mats. You cut old material into strips, and pushed them through the holes. This needlework holder screwed onto the table with a pincushion on top. These very old scissors were made by the blacksmith. This is a crimping machine, and these two sewing machines are 100 and 140 years old. My mother had the first treadle in the village.

Pipe-smoking was the thing in my days. This pipe came from the 1851 exhibition, and takes apart. It took one ounce of tobacco, and my father bought it for sixpence when he was working at Wantage. You went into The Bull on Saturday night and if you bought a pint of beer you got a pipe, put half an ounce of tobacco in, lit it and passed it round the pub. When they had all had enough it was red hot, and took nearly half a pint of beer to put it out. These are French pipes from the prisoners of war. When each pipe-smoker died I got his pipe for the Museum. Albert Tinson couldn't get enough tobacco, so he smoked his tea ration. This is a clay churchwarden's pipe. Every month there was a meeting at The Bull Inn to square up the Workhouse bills. They charged £3 for letting the room. The bills were for food for the poor people and wool for them to make clothes. The Vicar was expected to find beer and tobacco for the meeting, and the churchwarden had to provide the pipes. This spittoon came from The Lamb Inn.

Here are some interesting things all to do with lighting. A rush-light holder — you lit the end and pushed it up as it burned. The tallow dip was made of beeswax and mutton fat. This is a mould for making six candles, and here is a candle box and snuffers. A tinder box — flint and steel and cotton wool for lighting the fire. Once I heard my grandmother saying she couldn't get her fire going so I took my tongs and got a hot coal from a neighbour and carried it to her house. This lamp couldn't be turned over and was used as a night light. This baker's lamp was shifted about in the oven when the bread was baking. And this is what is called a lantern nowadays, but the proper name is lanthorn, because as you can see its sides are horn, not glass.

Most of the things I have collected to do with village trades are in the next room, but there are a few here too. Here are some very sharp knives used by the doctor, and this fleam stick which he used to bleed you. The larger knives were used by the vet. This is the doctor's wooden pillbox. This is Mr Booker's old cobbler's bench and this is the lapswing he held in on his knees for hammering on. This wooden vice he also held between his knees for sewing, and the bigger one belonged to the saddler. These are some of the village constable's tools, his staff and his rattle. If there was a fire he went all round the village with his rattle to get help. This is the whistle he carried in his belt, and his shackles. And these are two man traps used in the woods to catch poachers. Very nasty things. My grandmother told me that once the keeper was caught in one.

This is the staff which belonged to the Red, White and Blue Club, which I have spoken about earlier, telling how on Whit Tuesday each steward carried one round the village with a bunch of flowers on top. And this is the red ribbon my great uncle Job Farmer wore round his knee when he danced as Captain of the Morris men.

Now we'll move into the second room. We'll start with the blacksmith. What the old blacksmiths used to do! Handmade nails, handmade nuts and bolts! The wives and children made the small nails on a handmill.

Here are some very old locks and keys — large ones — used on barns. They had to be strong because poor people would break in to steal some corn to make a little bit of bread.

Next is the door furniture, handles and catches and fastenings. They weren't made by the hundred in those days. The blacksmith made the design you wanted, and you asked him to suit your particular door. Some of the designs were very nice indeed. The window furniture has lovely work in it. They were mostly iron window frames in those days.

This is a nice collection of decorated hinges. First the straight strap, then the T-L, very heavy but rather pretty. Then the Frog or Cock-Head as it was called. Then the H, the H-L and the Butterfly.

These wooden shovels were used chiefly for mixing the cattle feed with chaff and swedes.

We come to the tools next — I've a large collection of those. You had to make your own paint, so you got some oil and powder and red lead and ground them up. This hand grinder is an old pebble with a flat side, which you rubbed single-handed or double-handed. You can see some of the red lead still on it. Later somebody invented this paint mill. You turn the handle and the little cog turns the mill rod — the same idea as the corn mill. You had to control it, I should think, so the paint didn't come over the edge.

Wheelwrights' tools and carpenters' tools — what a tremendous lot, and all different! What shall I start with? Here is the long-handled adze. These are spokeshaves, which the carpenter and blacksmith made together. The chisels and gouges have handles of ash wood. I've got my first little hammer here somewhere, but I expect I can't find it — that one Father gave me when I was small. I could use it at twelve months.

These are the augers and gimlets, which can go with any sort of different tools. Then the clamps. I forget what this particular one is as the wheelwright never told me its name, but you screw it up to make handles of different sizes, smaller or bigger.

Now the wheelwright's braces. I've just got this wooden one which John Clark of the Bakery gave me. Beautiful it is, brass and beechwood, with an ebony handle. These chisels are all split at the ends with so much hammering.

My grandfather got logs of wood to make lathes called battens, to hang the roofing slates on. We didn't have the saws we have today, so we had to split them. This tool which is called a fromard was used by old George Willis, my Grampy. The hurdle-maker had a bigger fromard, and used it with a tommyhawk to peck out the wood, instead of a hammer and chisel, as he couldn't go to that trouble.

This is the Mill Peck. See how it chases in the mill stones. Bottom and top stones had the same grooves in them, and as they went round and round, so they smashed the corn.

Now I think I'll go on to this nice little bowl made

of mahogany and oak, which is a plumb-bob level.

Now the mason's tools. This was my natter, well-worn like me, with my name stamp on. Apple wood, with an ash handle — made it myself. The trick in that handle is that you pick it up and feel for a certain flat place for your finger, then you don't have to find the right place to beat the chisel.

This is the mason's chisel, a mallet-headed one, much smoother, so you don't knock the mallet about too much.

Here you've got your mason's trowels for laying on the mortar, and here are your slate picks. There's a hole in the pick, and you fasten it with a wooden peg to hang onto the next slate. Today they just put a nail in the slate.

These are the mason's hammers to chop stone, I've got a lot of these, and here are the slater's tools. You put a peg in and hang him on, and he comes behind the batten, then when you've got the plaster on he's in the way, so go along with the nippers — snip! snip! — cutting the pegs off.

This is the chard, for cutting and chasing a big block of stone, and this is a kibble for pecking knobs off stones.

Here are the plumb-bobs for stone-wallers, and here's the mason's level with a little bob made in moulds on string. This is a wooden plumb-rule. Dry walls get smaller as they go up and you've got to get it just right. There were battens each side of the wall, so it makes it narrower at the top. All this is out of date now, of course. There were a tremendous lot of things to do then.

Quarrying — look at the wheels of this old truck! I wonder what donkey pulled the stones out with that. It goes back to the middle of the last century.

This is an unusual tool — I think a lot of it. My mother took it along to hang the kettle on to make the tea when she went lessing. She worked from eight in the morning till five at night. A long job.

This is a carrot-digger. Until two hundred years ago there were no turnips or swedes, but great big carrots, so you needed a long tool for digging them up for the cattle. We called them Horse Carrots. Anything big gets called Horse, like Horse Mushrooms.

Here's something very interesting, a knife used by my father's uncle. You take a bunch of blackberry briars and cut them there and there and there, three sides with the knife, and pull them through a ring to get the thorns off. Then you use your knife to split and even up the bundles. The beehive maker used these blackberry ties to lace up. The straw was not plaited, just pulled up straight.

These Saxon knives we found when we dug out the swimming pool are just the same as my father's uncle's knife — see them side by side. A bone from a sheep's leg made the handle. It just proves they were doing the same thing in Saxon times as my great-uncle did.

Here are some more Saxon things — a nice comb, wonderful decorations, two bone needles, and here's a stone lamp. You put oil in the hole and hung the wick out.

These are the bells of a harness, I expect.

The oldest tool I have is this flint axe — see how

highly polished it is. And here's a bit of coal with a fernleaf pattern on it — a fossil, of course, about three hundred million years ago. Before we dug the swimming pool we found nine Saxon graves. Jim Farmer's family have got a paper about it somewhere.

This is a cheese press. In our time you just made a little bit for yourselves, not to sell, as in earlier times at the cheese and butter Cross at Langford This butter churn was used to make a small quantity for yourselves only, during the First World War, for instance.

These horses' nosebags were made of coconut and the saddler then sewed on the leather bottom and handle. All these little jobs have gone now. I remember so often seeing the horses tossing them up in the air to get the last bit out, and wondering who learned them that. They just found out, I expect.

This sieve, to sift the dust out of the chaff, was made of split cane. The nearest basket-maker was Bayliss, of Burford. I had to go sometimes to take baskets to be mended. You see the grooves for your thumbs to hold.

This is a wooden drainpipe. I remember a time up at Broughton Mill when the rats made a hole in one and it flooded a field which was owned by another man. They quarrelled, but came to an agreement with a new drainpipe.

This branding iron for cattle and sheep has CLARK on it. Mr Clark from the Bakery gave it to me. This poleaxe came from the butcher. Do you see two little holes? The hair went in one and came out the other. Nasty job — they don't do it like that now.

This is an oxtail skinner, for skinning tails for oxtail soup.

These leather horseshoes were used when you mowed the lawn, of course, and the brewer used them on his horses, too, when the roads were slippery.

These are steel quoits. Every pub had its quoit bed, and we boys would get a penny for watering it to keep it moist, so that the pegs stuck in.

Here's a horse scraper to get the sweat off the working horses, and this comb with all those little teeth is a bull comb for when you wanted to get them tidy for Shows. Very short hair the pedigree Shorthorn cattle had, like Garne's. The Cotswold cattle were long-haired.

This breaking bit has a tassel on it for the horse to play with while he's getting used to it.

These huge scissors are for Cotswold pedigree sheep. Their coats were down to the ground and you had to wedge them up to shear them.

A file for horses' teeth. Twelve horses Garne used to work. This is a bull-ringing outfit pincers, needle and ring. And this is a branding iron belonging to Thomas Dodd, a farmer at Broughton. I remember him when I was a boy.

This is for scratching bristles off the pig, after you'd burned them. It's got a hook on the other side to get the hoofs off. When they were hot they came off easily. The butcher who killed the pig hung it up to cool, and came back the next day to cut it up just how you wanted it, big or small joints.

Here are some sheep bells. Each makes a different sound, and the shepherd would know his own sound, and if he heard them ringing gently he knew his sheep were all right, but if there was a lot of rattling and clanging, he knew something like a dog or a fox was worrying them. The shepherd would be out in the foggy dark, listening hard all over Filkins Down. There were no hedges then, so the sheep travelled far.

These are yokes — much safer than collars. If an animal wore a collar he might hang himself, and the more he jumped about, the worse he got. He couldn't with a yoke, because it can't close up.

This is a wooden cowbell. You heard them all ringing when the cows were coming in at night.

This is a scraper, used when you singed off the fat part of the sheepskin, and made parchment with what was left. Very old.

An old bodkin, and a flute — played in the band in church before they had organs. Had to go, or you'd have the parson on your track. And a fiddle too. Fiddler John Farmer played for dances, as well. Jim Farmer played the cornet, and I started off with it, and finished up with the big bass. We had to buy new instruments after the First War as they were all worse for wear. You see, we were keen to start the Band up again.

This is the farrier's box. He took a candle with him and his apron, as well as his tools. This is a docking knife for horses, which the vet from Lechlade gave to me for the Museum, and said he'd never use the thing any more as it was a horrible job. I can't see any point in doing it, myself. What looks better than a nice tail on a horse, flowing out behind? It helps guide him, too.

This is a shoulder stick, with the rush basket you

carried on it, made from the rushes which grew in the river. We men used to carry them to work with us.

This is a seed fiddle. You had it strapped round your neck, and you pulled the string back and forth to sow the seed.

I could make a long story out of this part of the Museum, but I think I'd better stop here.

POSTSCRIPT

This book is based on several sources. The two principal ones are George's memoirs which he wrote in 1958, and the many hours of conversation which have been recorded with George in his later years. At various points in this story he conveys his sense of a gradual and somewhat depressing decline in the quality of village life. Often in conversation he remarks: "Nothing happens any more." By this he means that when he walks around the village he misses the bustle, activity and noise of the past. No cows are being driven to be milked, horses to be shod or pigs to be ringed; no bullocks cool off in the river after unloading their wagons. No one bowls a cartwheel down the street to be bonded by the blacksmith or saws coffin boards in his front yard; there are no smells from the bakery, no pedlars' stalls or games of marbles in the dust outside The Lamb. In George's youth working and domestic life spilled out of overcrowded cottages and cramped sheds onto the street, and Filkins was always on show like a line of washing. Billy Puffitt, living in public under a hedge, evoked no surprise.

There were three threads that bound any village together, and all stemmed from the relative isolation of most communities until after the Second World War. Firstly, local industry and commerce was geared to satisfy the everyday needs of local people. Bread, ale, cabbages, pokers, mats, nails, eggs, door handles were produced by and for the villagers. Secondly, isolation meant that most people were employed in and around the village, especially on the land, except at times of extreme unemployment, as George has described. This created a hierarchy of master and man which gave the village a sense of unity, and increased the feeling of interdependence. Thirdly, in the absence of state health and social services, most extra-family provision came from neighbours.

Welfare clubs and benefit societies with their elaborate rules and rituals were run by and for the villagers themselves. Even the village school, although part of the educational system, was an idiosyncratic element of village life as George describes it, which accounted for the somewhat unorthodox ending to his own school career. The Doctor ran his practice more or less as he saw fit, and it seems that to all intents and purposes the Vicar *was* the church.

Now there are great differences. Increased mobility, coupled with higher levels of material expectation, have meant that local needs are no longer satisfied by local suppliers. A pair of shoes made to fit either foot is not now acceptable; you can no longer hire a bicycle or get your coffin made in Filkins. As a consequence, local businesses have either closed or turned to wider markets. Of the two remaining pubs, one now operates chiefly as a popular restaurant for visitors from outside the village. The blacksmith no longer shoes horses or mends saucepans, but makes ornamental gates, weathercocks and fire-irons, which find a ready market over a wide area. By contrast the Post Office Stores is unique in being the only village shop-cum-post office for miles around. It is perhaps close in character to the shops of George's day, since in spite of competition from supermarkets in nearby towns it supplies many of the staple needs of the village, especially those of the elderly. It is an important social centre, and it is *there*, almost on the doorstep, for the instant, essential and unexpected need.

The village has attracted new businesses, mostly those that can benefit from the rural Cotswold setting, or are operated by people who simply want to live and work in such a village. There is a small woollen mill, a picture gallery, a firm of landscape architects, a rush and cane weaver, a furniture restorer, a stonemason, a potter and a firm of stone slate roofers. In 1985 there were thirty-one individual businesses operating in or from Filkins. They do not supply the village like the old businesses, since their customers come from far and wide, and so they are less visible and would seem to touch the lives of local people less. They do provide some employment, and attract visitors who bring custom to existing businesses like the pubs and the smithy. But as they establish themselves they, in their turn, gradually become part of the familiar fabric of social life, whether as talking points, meeting places or centres of activity which bring a new direction and dynamism to Filkins.

There is less decline in social and community life than George suggests, albeit there was a slump following the Second World War. One factor might be that today women play a much greater part in what goes on outside the home than they did in George's time, having more leisure, which affects the nature as well as the viability of village activities. The school has been closed, the band and welfare club have gone, and the church no longer holds the powerful central position it once did. Families are perhaps more private, life maybe is conducted more discreetly between four walls. You could say that the village street is principally a means of getting from A to B, and somewhere to put the car and the dustbin, and that people keep themselves to themselves and sit indoors watching television instead of taking part in local life.

This is questionable. Children cycle ceaselessly up and down the streets, teenage groups sit on walls or in the bus shelter (an unofficial social centre); people of all ages jam up the Post Office Stores and gather at garden gates *talking*. The Bowls Club has just celebrated its fiftieth anniversary, extended its pavilion, plays matches over a wide area and has an impressive regalia. The Football Club has long had its own colours and gear, and hopes soon to buy its own pitch. This year the Women's Institute marked its fortieth year, and recently surveyed the parish as part of the national Domesday project. The Handbell Ringers give performances and compete all over the district. The Over-Sixties Club flourishes. A group interested in acting and entertaining is in the process of being formed. The Village Hall, which George helped to build, has been extended, and is increasingly in demand for dances, drama, shows, sales, and a mothers and toddlers group, as well as for the meetings of the various organizations, and for private social functions. Doctors attend the surgery four times a week; the outdoor swimming pool and children's playground have been refurbished. To maintain interest,

199

all village organizations and activities have to meet high standards.

There is still a network of neighbourliness, albeit different from in George's day when his father organized a team of men to fetch water from the brook to beat the drought. Support, sympathy and practical help is perhaps more on an individual basis. George himself, now in his hundredth year, receives neighbours with flasks of soup and slices of ginger cake, to sit by his fire and listen once again to his stories, with always a fresh item of information (maddening to the editors of this now-completed book). "Those clap-nets I telled you about for catching sparrows — I used to knit them myself when I could lay my hands on the money to buy the string. Came from Witney. Tricky job it was!"

All in all, there is perhaps as much village life as there has ever been. It is not as central to survival as it was, but it does mean that Filkins will continue to thrive. There are still village characters and village affairs for future George Swinfords to chronicle.

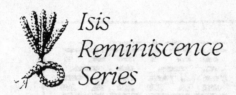

Isis
Reminiscence
Series

The ISIS Reminiscence Series has been developed with the older reader in mind. Well-loved in their own right, these titles are chosen for their memory-evoking content.

Fred Archer	**A Lad of Evesham Vale**
Fred Archer	**Poachers Pie***
Fred Archer	**The *Countryman Cottage* Life Book**
Fred Archer	**When Village Bells Were Silent**
Eileen Balderson	**Backstairs Life in a Country House**
H. E. Bates	**In The Heart of the Country**
Anna Blair	**Tea at Miss Cranston's**
Derek Brock	**Small Coals and Smoke Rings**
Peter Davies	**A Corner of Paradise**
Alice Thomas Ellis	**A Welsh Childhood**
Ida Gandy	**A Wiltshire Childhood**
Lesley Lewis	**The Private Life of a Country House**
Venetia Murray	**Where Have All the Cowslips Gone?**

*Available in Hardback and Softback.

Isis
Reminiscence
Series

* Available in Hardback and Softback.

BIOGRAPHY AND AUTOBIOGRAPHY

Lord Abercromby	**Childhood Memories**
Margery Allingham	**The Oaken Heart**
Hilary Bailey	**Vera Brittain**
Winifred Beechey	**The Reluctant Samaritan**
P. Y. Betts	**People Who Say Goodbye**
Christabel Bielenberg	**The Road Ahead**
Kitty Black	**Upper Circle**
Denis Constanduros	**My Grandfather**
Dalai Lama	**Freedom in Exile**
W. H. Davies	**Young Emma**
Phil Drabble	**A Voice in the Wilderness**
Joyce Fussey	**Calf Love**
Valerie Garner	**Katherine: The Duchess of Kent**
Gillian Gill	**Agatha Christie**
Jon & Rumer Godden	**Two Under the Indian Sun**
William Golding	**The Hot Gates**
Michael Green	**The Boy Who Shot Down an Airship**
Michael Green	**Nobody Hurt in Small Earthquake**
Unity Hall & Ingrid Seward	
	Royalty Revealed
Brian Hoey	**The New Royal Court**
Ilse, Countess von Bredow	
	Eels With Dill Sauce
Clive James	**Falling Towards England**
Clive James	**May Week Was in June**

BIOGRAPHY AND AUTOBIOGRAPHY

Paul James	Margaret
Paul James	Princess Alexandra
Julia Keay	The Spy Who Never Was
Dorothy Brewer Kerr	The Girls Behind the Guns
John Kerr	Queen Victoria's Scottish Diaries
Margaret Lane	The Tale of Beatrix Potter
T. E. Lawrence	Revolt in the Desert
Bernard Levin	The Way We Live Now
Margaret Lewis	Ngaio Marsh
Vera Lynn	Unsung Heroines
Jeanine McMullen	A Small Country Living Goes On
Gavin Maxwell	Ring of Bright Water
Ronnie Knox Mawer	Tales From a Palm Court
Peter Medawar	Memoir of a Thinking Radish
Jessica Mitford	Hons and Rebels
Christopher Nolan	Under the Eye of the Clock (A)
Christopher Ralling	The Kon Tiki Man
Wng Cdr Paul Richey	Fighter Pilot
Martyn Shallcross	The Private World of Daphne Du Maurier
Frank and Joan Shaw	We Remember the Blitz
Frank and Joan Shaw	We Remember the Home Guard
Joyce Storey	Our Joyce
Robert Westall	The Children of the Blitz
Ben Wicks	The Day They Took the Children (A)

(A) Large Print books also available in Audio.

WORLD WAR II

Margery Allingham	The Oaken Heart
Paul Brickhill	The Dam Busters
Josephine Butler	Cyanide In My Shoe
Reinhold Eggers	Escape From Colditz
Joyce Grenfell	The Time of My Life
John Harris	Dunkirk
Vera Lynn	We'll Meet Again (A)
Vera Lynn	Unsung Heroines
Frank Pearce	Sea War
Maude Pember Reeves	Round About a Pound a Week
Wing Cdr Paul Richey	Fighter Pilot
Frank and Joan Shaw	We Remember the Blitz
Frank and Joan Shaw	We Remember The Homeguard
William Sparks	The Last of the Cockleshell Heroes
Anne Valery	Talking About the War
Robert Westall	Children of the Blitz
Ben Wicks	The Day They Took the Children (A)

POETRY

Felicity Kendall	The Family Poetry Book
	Long Remembered: Narrative Poems

COOKERY

Jennifer Davies	The Victorian Kitchen

REFERENCE AND DICTIONARIES

The Lion Concise Bible Encyclopedia
The Longman English Dictionary
The Longman Medical Dictionary

(A) Large Print books also available in Audio.

GENERAL NON-FICTION

Estelle Catlett	**Track Down Your Ancestors**
Eric Delderfield	**Eric Delderfield's Bumper Book of True Animal Stories**
Phil Drabble	**One Man and His Dog**
Caroline Elliot	**The BBC Book of Royal Memories 1947-1990**
Jonathan Goodman	**The Lady Killers**
Joan Grant	**The Owl on the Teapot**
Anita Guyton	**Healthy Houseplants A-Z**
Helene Hanff	**Letters From New York**
Dr Richard Lacey	**Safe Shopping, Safe Cooking, Safe Eating**
Sue Lawley	**Desert Island Discussions**
Doris Lessing	**Particularly Cats and More Cats**
Martin Lloyd-Elliott	**City Ablaze**
Vera Lynn	**We'll Meet Again**
Richard Mabey	**Home Country**
Frank Muir & Denis Norden	
	You Have My Word
Shiva Naipual	**An Unfinished Journey**
Colin Parsons	**Encounters With the Unknown**
John Pilger	**A Secret Country**
R W F Poole	**A Backwoodsman's Year**
Valerie Porter	**Faithful Companions**
Sonia Roberts	**The Right Way to Keep Pet Birds**
Yvonne Roberts	**Animal Heroes**
Anne Scott-James	**Gardening Letters to My Daughter**
Anne Scott-James and Osbert Lancaster	
	The Pleasure Garden
Les Stocker	**The Hedgehog and Friends**

GENERAL NON-FICTION